HUMOROU

HUMOROUS QUOTATIONS

DES MacHALE

MERCIER PRESS

MERCIER PRESS
PO Box 5, 5 French Church Street, Cork
16 Hume Street, Dublin 2

© Des MacHale

ISBN 1 85635 076 2

A CIP is available for this book from the British Library.

10 9 8 7 6 5 4 3 2

*This book is dedicated
to my brother Benny
with affection*

Printed in Ireland by Colour Books Ltd.

Contents

Contents

Introduction

Over the last twenty years or so, I have been collecting humorous quotations from books, magazines, newspapers, radio, television, films, records, word of mouth, and any other source that one can possibly imagine. This book is the result of my labours and it has given me a lot of fun.

A good humorous quotation in my opinion should have several qualities.

i)   First of all it should be funny – it should provoke laughter or at least a smile. Too many books of humorous quotations are shamelessly padded with substandard material that is not even remotely funny. I humbly submit that this book is different.

ii) It should be short and pithy, for brevity is the soul of wit: the average quotation in this book has about fourteen words, but I have not resisted the temptation to include just a few longer quotes of exceptional merit.

iii) It should be free-standing i.e. it must be independent of the context in which it arises. This rather stringent requirement will undoubtedly eliminate some old favourites of yours and mine, but look at it this way – if the explanation of why a quotation is funny because of where it arises is actually longer than the quotation itself, is it really worth the bother?

For the convenience of speakers, writers and others who require humorous quotations to spice up their material, this book has been divided into twenty wide-ranging chapters and there is also an index listing all the quotations attributed to each individual. This naturally begs the question – who was the greatest wit of all time? I have thought long and hard on this question and I have found it virtually impossible to choose a single name – doubtless very few people would agree on a single choice. Putting my neck on the chopping block, the most I will risk is the following opinion.

Oscar Wilde was the greatest wit of the nineteenth century and Woody Allen is the greatest wit of the twentieth century. Wilde's wit was sophisticated and clever, while Allen's wit is hilarious and down to earth, but I find it impossible to separate them in terms of merit. Perhaps it is fitting that the prize be shared between the Irish and the Jews – the two wittiest races that have ever lived.

In the second flight I would place Mark Twain, Evelyn Waugh, Ambrose Bierce, George Ade, Steven Wright, Emo Philips, H.L. Mencken, Brendan Behan, Thomas Beecham, George Burns, Quentin Crisp, Noel Coward, Phyllis Diller, W.C. Fields, Dick Gregory, Spike Milligan, Groucho Marx, Joan Rivers, George Bernard Shaw, and Alexander Woollcott.

Honourable mention goes to the following: Robert Benchley, Max Beerbohm, Winston Churchill, Samuel Goldwyn, Bob Hope, Heinrich Heine, Samuel Johnson, Stephen Leacock, Ring Lardner, P.J. O'Rourke, Dorothy Parker, Rita Rudner, Sydney Smith, James Thurber and Lee Trevino.

I have not burdened the text with potted biographies of the contributors – not even birth dates or death dates, because such information is largely irrelevant to the humour, and in any case can easily be looked up elsewhere if needed. I honestly believe that this collection of well over two thousand humorous quotations that you, lucky reader, are about to immerse yourself in, is the best such collection ever assembled. I believe this so strongly that if you can provide me with a better and funnier collection, I will eat it, without seasoning.

Enjoy!

DES MacHALE
Cork, May, 1994

Art

1:1   Abstract art is a product of the untalented, sold by the unprincipled, to the utterly bewildered.

Al Capp

1:2   I inherited a painting and a violin which turned out to be a Rembrandt and a Stradivarius. Unfortunately Rembrandt made lousy violins and Stradivarius was a terrible painter.

Tommy Cooper

1:3   Anyone who sees and paints a sky green and fields blue ought to be sterilised.

Adolf Hitler

1:4   Which painting in the National Gallery would I save if there was a fire? The one nearest the door of course.

George Bernard Shaw

1:5   The only thoroughly original ideas I have ever heard Mr Whistler express have had reference to his own superiority as a painter over painters greater than himself.

Oscar Wilde

1:6   She looks like the Venus de Milo; she is very old, has no teeth, and has white spots on her yellow skin.

Heinrich Heine

1:7   She is one of those ladies who pursue culture in bands, as though it were dangerous to meet it alone.

Edith Wharton

1:8   There is only one difference between a madman and me. I am not mad.

Salvador Dali

1:9   He was as ugly as a gargoyle hewn by a drunken stonemason for the adornment of a Methodist Chapel in one of the vilest suburbs of Leeds or Wigan.

Max Beerbohm

1:10   You ask me, Sir, for a suitable institution to which you propose to leave your paintings. May I suggest an asylum for the blind?

James McNeill Whistler

1:11   I don't understand anything about the ballet. All I know is that during the intervals the ballerinas stink like horses.

Anton Chekhov

1:12   Post-Impressionist drawing is on the level of an untaught child of seven or eight years old, the sense of colour of a tea-tray painter, the method of a schoolboy who wipes his fingers on a slate after spitting on them.

Wilfred Blunt

1:13   I am lonesome. They are all dying. I have hardly a warm personal enemy left.

James McNeill Whistler

1:14   If it sells, it's art.

Frank Lloyd

1:15   Many excellent cooks are spoilt by going into the arts.

Paul Gauguin

1:16   All the arts in America are a gigantic racket run by unscrupulous men for unhealthy women.

Thomas Beecham

1:17   Can it be mere coincidence that so many of the best Post-Impressionists are Poles?

Patrick Murray

1:18   There is nothing on earth more terrible than English music, except English painting.

Heinrich Heine

1:19   There is only one difference between a madman and me. The madman thinks he is sane. I know I am mad.

Salvador Dali

1:20   'Burn the museums!' This old revolutionary slogan can now be realised by the museums themselves. A museum set on fire would today attract the usual crowd that visits its exhibitions. It calls not for the end of art but for the expansion of art institutions to include the medium of combustion.

Harold Rosenberg

1:21   This is either a forgery or a damn clever original.

Frank Sullivan

1:22   Gerald Kelly made a last desperate attempt to persuade the world he was an artist by marrying a model. But this device deceived nobody.

Alastair Crowley

1:23   The goitrous, torpid and squinting husks provided by Matisse in his sculpture are worthless except as tactful decorations for a mental home.

Percy Wyndham-Lewis

1:24   Mr Whistler, with all his faults, was never guilty of writing a line of poetry.

Oscar Wilde

1:25   Dada's art is just turpentine intoxication.

Marcel Duchamp

1:26   The preponderance of women and homosexuals in the arts today signifies only the scurrying of rats near a dying body.

Shulamith Firestone

Business and Money

2:1   I've been rich and I've been poor – rich is better.

Sophie Tucker

2:2   If you would like to know the value of money, go and try to borrow some.

Benjamin Franklin

2:3   I've got all the money I'll ever need if I die by four o'clock this afternoon.

Henny Youngman

2:4   October. This is one of the peculiarly dangerous months to speculate in stocks. Other dangerous months are July, January, September, April, November, May, March, June, December, August and February.

Mark Twain

2:5   When I was young I used to think that money was the most important thing in life. Now that I am old, I know it is.

Oscar Wilde

2:6   I owe much; I have nothing; the rest I leave to the poor.

Francois Rabelais

2:7   A lot of people become pessimists from financing optimists.

C.T. Jones

2:8   Money is just the poor man's credit card.

Marshall McLuhan

2:9   A man who has a million dollars is as well off as if he were rich.

Cleveland Amory

2:10   Dear *Reader's Digest*, we hardly know each other, yet I have been selected from so many millions to enter your free contest in which I may win £25,000. You have made me very happy.

Miles Kington

2:11   My luck is so bad that if I bought a cemetery, people would stop dying.

Ed Furgol

2:12   Undermine the entire economic structure of society by leaving the pay toilet door ajar so the next person can get in free.

Taylor Meade

2:13   I always arrive late at the office, but I make up for it by leaving early.

Charles Lamb

2:14   A verbal contract isn't worth the paper it's written on.

Samuel Goldwyn

2:15   It is only by not paying one's bills that one can hope to live in the memory of the commercial classes.

Oscar Wilde

2:16   Money can't buy you happiness, but it does bring you a more pleasant form of misery.

Spike Milligan

2:17   The light at the end of the tunnel is just the light of an oncoming train.

Robert Lowell

2:18   When I asked my accountant if anything could get me out of the mess I am in now, he thought for a long time. 'Yes,' he said, 'death would help'.

Robert Morley

2:19   They usually have two tellers in my local bank. Except when it's very busy, when they have one.

Rita Rudner

2:20   It is morally wrong to allow a sucker to keep his money.

W.C. Fields

2:21   Having a little inflation is like being a little bit pregnant.

Leon Henderson

2:22   Office Hours: 2 to 2.15 every other Wednesday.

George S. Kaufman

2:23   I rob banks because that's where the money is.

Willie Sutton

2:24 Statistics indicate that as a result of overwork, modern executives are dropping like flies on the nation's golf courses.

Ira Wallach

2:25 We were allowed to accept gifts of flowers, candies, jewels, furs, yachts, castles – but never money.

Quentin Crisp

2:26 I always travel first-class on the train. It's the only way to avoid one's creditors.

Seymour Hicks

2:27 If only God would give me a clear sign! Like making a large deposit in my name at a Swiss bank.

Woody Allen

2:28 I haven't reported my missing credit card to the police because whoever stole it is spending less than my wife.

Ilie Nastase

2:29 The holy passion of friendship is of so sweet and steady and loyal and enduring a nature that it will last through a whole life-time, if not asked to lend money.

Mark Twain

2:30 You should always live within your income, even if you have to borrow to do so.

Josh Billings

2:31 All students of economics should learn about Marxism, just as all medical students should learn about venereal diseases.

C.K. Grant

2:32 Money is better than poverty, if only for financial reasons.

Woody Allen

2:33 One of the strangest things about life is that the poor, who need money the most, are the very ones that never have it.

Finley Peter Dunne

2:34 I wish that dear Karl could have spent some time acquiring capital instead of merely writing about it.

Jenny Marx

2:35 Blessed are the young, for they shall inherit the national debt.

Herbert Hoover

2:36   The first rule of business is – do other men for they would do you.

Charles Dickens

2:37   Any organisation is like a septic tank. The really big chunks always rise to the top.

John Imhoff

2:38   Never answer a letter until you get a second one on the same subject from the same person.

Michael O'Hagan

2:39   Tell your boss what you really think about him and the truth shall set you free.

Patrick Murray

2:40   I could have done the job myself in twenty minutes, but as things turned out I had to spend two days to find out why it had taken someone else three weeks to do it wrong.

J.L. McCafferty

2:41   If Bret Harte ever repaid a loan, the incident failed to pass into history.

Mark Twain

2:42   To make a long story short, there's nothing like having the boss walk in.

Doris Lilly

2:43   His insomnia was so bad, he couldn't sleep even during office hours.

Arthur Baer

2:44   What's the use of happiness? It can't buy you money.

Henny Youngman

2:45   Nothing is as irritating as the fellow who chats pleasantly to you while he's overcharging you.

Kin Hubbard

2:46   There are three easy ways of losing money – racing is the quickest, women the most pleasant, and farming the most certain.

Lord Amherst

2:47   Any man who has $10,000 left when he dies is a failure.

Errol Flynn

2:48   I don't owe a penny to a single soul – not counting trades-
men of course.

P.G. Wodehouse

2:49   I have enough money to last me the rest of my life – unless I
have to buy something.

Jackie Mason

2:50   There are worse things in life than death. Have you ever
spent an evening with an insurance salesman?

Woody Allen

2:51   God has mercifully withheld from humanity a foreknow-
ledge of what will sell.

Bernard Miles

2:52   I'm living so far beyond my income that we may almost be
said to be living apart.

e.e. Cummings

2:53   The government incomes policy is as significant as a blush
on a dead man's cheek.

Clive Jenkins

2:54   Today's payslip has more deductions than a Sherlock
Holmes story.

Raymond J. Cvikota

2:55   Don't tell my mother I work in an advertising agency. She
thinks I play the piano in a whorehouse.

Jacques Seguela

2:56   Business is often about killing your favourite children to
allow the others to succeed.

John Harvey-Jones

2:57   There was a time when a fool and his money were soon
parted, but now it happens to everybody.

Adlai Stevenson

2:58   If there is anyone to whom I owe money, I am prepared to
forget it if they are.

Errol Flynn

2:59   I want a one-armed economist so that the guy could never
make a statement and then say 'on the other hand ...'

Harry Truman

2:60   Don't get excited about a tax cut. It's like a mugger giving you back fare for a taxi.

Arnold Glasow

2:61   Money isn't everything, but it's a long way ahead of what comes next.

Edmund Stockdale

2:62   Here is a useful shopping tip: you can get a pair of shoes for £1 at bowling alleys.

Al Clethen

2:63   I get so tired of listening to one million dollars here, one million dollars there. It's so petty.

Imelda Marcos

2:64   I have never known an auctioneer to lie, unless it was absolutely necessary.

Josh Billings

2:65   There are three ways to lose money: on horses, women and engineers. Horses are the easiest, women the most fun and engineers the fastest.

Rolf Skar

2:66   A breakfast meeting is the most uncivilised idea I've ever heard of. If you're going to have a breakfast meeting it should be in bed with a beautiful woman.

Gordon White

2:67   Fire the whole purchasing department. They'd hire Einstein and then turn down his requisition for a blackboard.

Robert Townsend

2:68   I put the *Financial Times* on the floor and called my dog William over to pee on it. Wherever there was a mark I could do some trading.

Bob Beckman

2:69   All the great economic ills the world has known this century can be directly traced back to the London School of Economics.

N.M. Perrera

2:70   A billion here, a billion there and pretty soon you're talking about real money.

Everett Dirksen

2:71   Making a speech on economics is a bit like pissing down
        your leg. It seems hot to you but never to anyone else.

                                            Lyndon B. Johnson

2:72   I'd like to be rich enough so I could throw soap away after
        the letters are worn off.

                                            Andy Rooney

2:73   I was a lousy accountant. I always figured that if you came
        within eight bucks of what you needed you were doing OK.
        I made up the difference out of my own pocket.

                                            Bob Newhart

2:74   My formula for success is rise early, work late, and strike oil.

                                            Paul Getty

2:75   An economist's guess is as good as anybody else's.

                                            Will Rogers

2:76   When I was young I used to think that wealth and power
        would bring me happiness. I was right.

                                            Gahan Wilson

2:77   In the midst of life we are in debt.

                                            Ethel Mumford

2:78   Women prefer men who have something tender about them
        – especially legal tender.

                                            Kay Ingram

2:79   If all else fails, immortality can always be assured by a spec-
        tacular error.

                                            J.K. Galbraith

2:80   My husband once worked for a company where they had a
        merit pay system. After six months they told him that he
        owed the company money.

                                            Phyllis Diller

2:81   I am opposed to millionaires, but it would be dangerous to
        offer me the position.

                                            Mark Twain

2:82   One way to solve all the traffic problems would be to keep
        all the cars that aren't paid for off the streets.

                                            Will Rogers

2:83   I never pass an empty telephone box without pressing Button B. Button B has often been kind to me.

Joyce Cary

2:84   Avoid like the plague a clergyman who is also a business man.

Saint Jerome

2:85   I did not marry my wife because she had four million. I would have married her if she had only two million.

Charles Forte

2:86   One of the mysteries of human conduct is why adult men and women are ready to sign documents which they do not read, at the behest of salesmen they do not know, binding them to pay for articles they do not want, with money which they do not have.

Gerald Hurst

2:87   The best advice I was ever given was on my twenty-first birthday when my father said 'Son, here's a million dollars. Don't lose it'.

Larry Niven

2:88   Happiness is getting a bill you've already paid, so you can sit down and write a really nasty letter.

Peter Nero

2:89   My grandfather died in the great crash of 1929 – a stock-broker jumped out of a window and crushed him and his pushcart down below.

Mario Cuomo

2:90   The avoidance of taxes is the only intellectual pursuit that still carries any reward.

J.M. Keynes

2:91   Insufficient attention is given to real costs when installing university laboratory equipment. In some cases it would be cheaper not to install the equipment, but whenever it is needed to send each student in a separate chauffeur-driven Rolls-Royce to use the same equipment at another institution.

C.F. Carter

2:92 I'm very proud of my gold pocket watch. My grandfather, on his deathbed, sold me this watch.

Woody Allen

2:93 I worked my way up from nothing to a state of extreme poverty.

Groucho Marx

2:94 Those proud of keeping an orderly desk never know the thrill of finding something they thought they had irretrievably lost.

Helen Exley

2:95 I started out with nothing. I still have most of it.

Michael Davis

2:96 A good rule of thumb is if you've made it to thirty-five and your job still requires you to wear a name tag, you've probably made a serious vocational error.

Dennis Miller

2:97 It's so long since I've worked that one of my insurance stamps is worth more than a Penny Black.

Lenny Windsor

Drink and other Drugs

3:1 I am not a heavy drinker. I can sometimes go for hours without touching a drop.

Noel Coward

3:2 I drink therefore I am.

W.C. Fields

3:3 If I had my life to live over again, I'd live over a saloon.

W.C. Fields

3:4 A woman drove me to drink – and I hadn't even the courtesy to thank her.

W.C. Fields

3:5 I feel sorry for people who don't drink. They wake up in the morning and that's the best they are going to feel all day.

Dean Martin

3:6 Some American writers who have known each other for years have never met in the daytime or when both are sober.

James Thurber

3:7 An alcoholic is anyone you don't like who drinks more than you do.

Dylan Thomas

3:8 You're not drunk if you can lie on the floor without holding on.

Dean Martin

3:9 The drink in that pub is not fit for washing hearses.

Brendan Behan

3:10 Reality is an illusion created by a lack of alcohol.

N.F. Simpson

3:11 A tavern is a place where madness is sold by the bottle.

Jonathan Swift

3:12 May I suggest, sir, that if you want an impenetrable disguise for the fancy dress ball, that you go sober?

Samuel Foote

3:13   Work is the curse of the drinking classes.

Oscar Wilde

3:14   There are more old drunks than old doctors.

François Rabelais

3:15   My dad was the town drunk. Most of the time that's not so bad – but New York City?

Henny Youngman

3:16   I never drink water because of the disgusting things that fish do in it.

W.C. Fields

3:17   A cap of good acid costs five dollars and for that you can hear the Universal Symphony with God singing solo and the Holy Ghost on drums.

Hunter S. Thompson

3:18   I always keep a stimulant handy in case I see a snake – which I also keep handy.

W.C. Fields

3:19   He once had his toes amputated so he could stand closer to the bar.

Mike Harding

3:20   What contemptible scoundrel stole the cork from my lunch?

W.C. Fields

3:21   The trouble with him is that when he is not drunk he is sober.

W.B. Yeats

3:22   A debut is the first time a young girl is seen drunk in public.

F. Scott Fitzgerald

3:23   Cocaine is God's way of saying you're making too much money.

Robin Williams

3:24   I exercise strong self-control. I never drink anything stronger than gin before breakfast.

W.C. Fields

3:25   The AAAA is a new organisation for drunks who drive. Give them a call and they'll tow you away from the bar.

Martin Burden

3:26   Whiskey is by far the most popular of all the remedies that won't cure a cold.

Jerry Vale

3:27   The difference between a drunk and an alcoholic is that a drunk doesn't have to attend all those meetings.

Arthur J. Lewis

3:28   The Management of an Irish pub cannot be held responsible for any accidents which occur in the mad rush for the doors at closing time.

Tony Butler

3:29   A total abstainer is someone who abstains from everything except abstention.

Ambrose Bierce

3:30   He awoke with a severe hangover. His mouth felt as if it had been used as a latrine by some small animal.

Kingsley Amis

3:31   Your superego is that part of you which is soluble in alcohol.

Thomas L. Martin

3:32   I'd rather have a full bottle in front of me than a full frontal lobotomy.

Fred Allen

3:33   Perfection is such a nuisance that I often regret having cured myself of using tobacco.

Emile Zola

3:34   I once shook hands with Pat Boone and my whole right side sobered up.

Dean Martin

3:35   I can't die until the government finds a safe place to bury my liver.

Phil Harris

3:36   People keep warning me not to smoke too much, but I gotta. It's a matter of principle, like who's running my life – me or the *Reader's Digest*?

Dick Gregory

3:37   I got thrown out of Alcoholics Anonymous because when the other clients saw me they thought they were having the DTs.

Dave Dutton

3:38   There is nothing wrong with sobriety in moderation.

John Ciardi

3:39   Women add zest to the unlicenced hours.

Allen D. Thomas

3:40   A Temperance Hotel! You might as well speak of a celibate brothel.

George Tyrrell

3:41   Cocaine isn't habit forming. I should know because I've been taking it for years.

Tallulah Bankhead

3:42   I went into hospital for a liver transplant and boy was I unlucky! They gave me Oliver Reed's.

Lenny Windsor

3:43   My pappy told me never to bet my bladder against a brewery.

Lane Kirkland

3:44   The reason I drink is because when I'm sober I think I'm Eddie Fisher.

Dean Martin

3:45   Actually, it only takes one drink to get me drunk. The trouble is, I can't remember if it's the thirteenth or the fourteenth.

George Burns

3:46   I never smoked a cigarette until I was nine.

H.L. Mencken

3:47   You can tell German wine from vinegar by the label.

Mark Twain

3:48   It's not the taste of water I object to. It's the after effects.

Ronald Knox

3:49   I love drink, so long as it isn't in moderation.

Geoffrey Madan

3:50   I have been advised by the best medical authority, at my age, not to attempt to give up alcohol.

W.C. Fields

3:51   Never sit on a hard chair after drinking port.

H.J. Bidder

3:52   For a bad hangover take the juice of two quarts of whiskey.

Eddie Condon

3:53   Moonshine corn liquor has been known to stop the victim's watch, snap his suspenders and crack his glass eye right across.

Irvin Cobb

3:54   One day recently a man called out to me from the other side of the street asking me for the price of a drink. I beckoned him to come over for it and he waved me away. This has to be the Everest of laziness.

Jeffrey Bernard

3:55   I know I'm drinking myself to a slow death, but I'm in no hurry.

Robert Benchley

3:56   Wordsworth's standard of intoxication was miserably low.

J.H. Shorthouse

3:57   I distrust camels, and anyone else who can go a week without a drink.

Joe E. Lewis

3:58   If you drink, don't drive. Don't even putt.

Dean Martin

3:59   Health is what my friends are always drinking before they fall down.

Phyllis Diller

3:60   I smoke 10 to 15 cigars a day – at my age I have to hold on to something.

George Burns

Education

4:1   'Whom are you?' he said, for he had been to night school.
George Ade

4:2   My problems all started with my early education. I went to a school for mentally disturbed teachers.
Woody Allen

4:3   Educational television should be absolutely forbidden. It can only lead to unreasonable disappointment when your child discovers that the letters of the alphabet do not leap up out of books and dance around with royal-blue chickens.
Fran Lebowitz

4:4   Anyone who has been to an English public school will always feel comparatively at home in prison.
Evelyn Waugh

4:5   I took a speed reading course and read *War and Peace* in twenty minutes. It's about Russia.
Woody Allen

4:6.   I can speak Esperanto like a native.
Spike Milligan

4:7   I speak twelve languages – English is the bestest.
Stefan Bergman

4:8   My act is very educational. I heard a man leaving the other night saying 'Well, that's taught me a lesson'.
Ken Dodd

4:9   I wish that people who have difficulty in communicating would just shut up about it.
Tom Lehrer

4:10   If a man is a fool, you don't train him out of being a fool by sending him to university. You merely turn him into a trained fool, ten times more dangerous.
Desmond Bagley

4:11 'You will all write an essay on "self-indulgence". There will be a prize of half a crown for the longest essay, irrespective of any possible merit.' From then on all was silence until the break.

Evelyn Waugh

4:12 Never attribute to malice that which can be adaquately explained by straightforward stupidity.

J.C. Collins

4:13 The average Ph.D thesis is nothing but the transference of bones from one graveyard to the other.

J.F. Dobie

4:14 An intellectual is someone who has found something more interesting than sex.

Edgar Wallace

4:15 A lecture is a process by which the notes of the professor become the notes of the students without passing through the minds of either.

R.K. Rathbun

4:16 Let me protest against recent attacks on the fagging system at public schools. In all my four years I can recall only eleven deaths from fagging.

J.B. Morton

4:17 A man who has never gone to school may steal from a freight car; but if he has a university education, he may steal the whole railroad.

Theodore Roosevelt

4:18 Dublin University contains the cream of Ireland – rich and thick.

Samuel Beckett

4:19 I expect you'll be becoming a schoolmaster, sir. That's what most of the gentlemen does, sir, that gets sent down for indecent behaviour.

Evelyn Waugh

4:20 I don't hold with bilingualism. English was good enough for Jesus Christ.

Ralph Melnyk

4:21   Violence is the repartee of the illiterate.

Alan Brien

4:22   I cheated in the final of my metaphysics examination. I
       looked into the soul of the boy sitting next to me.

Woody Allen

4:23   I acquired such skill in reading Latin and Greek that I could
       take a page of either, and distinguish which language it was
       by merely glancing at it.

Stephen Leacock

4:24   A college graduate returned home from his twenty-fifth
       class reunion and said to his wife – 'My classmates have all
       gotten so fat and bald they didn't even recognise me'.

Bennett Cerf

4:25   Trinity College Cambridge is like a dead body in a high state
       of putrefaction. The only interest is the worms that come out
       of it.

Lytton Strachey

4:26   Harvard is a storehouse of knowledge because the freshmen
       bring so much in and the graduates take so little out.

Charles W. Eliot

4:27   I used to keep my college room-mate from reading my
       personal mail by hiding it in her textbooks.

Joan Welsh

4:28   The ablative absolute is an ancient form of grammatical error
       much admired by modern scholars.

Ambrose Bierce

4:29   We spend the first twelve months of our children's lives
       teaching them to walk and talk and the next twelve years
       telling them to sit down and shut up.

Phyllis Diller

4:30   Loaded firearms were strictly forbidden at St Trinians to all
       but Sixth Formers.

Timothy Shy

4:31   Ignorance is like a delicate exotic fruit; touch it and the
       bloom is gone.

Oscar Wilde

4:32 He can barely read and write – Eton, of course.

Lawrence Durrell

4:33 'Shut up', he explained.

Ring Lardner

4:34 When Lord Berners returned, many years later, to visit his old school, he was astonished to observe nothing but smiling faces – only to learn that it was a school no more and that the building was a lunatic asylum.

Arthur Marshall

4:35 He who can does – he who cannot, teaches.

George Bernard Shaw

4:36 In the first place God made idiots; that was for practice; then he made school boards.

Mark Twain

4:37 It is a pity that Chawser, who had geneyus, was so unedicated; he's the wuss speller I know of.

Artemus Ward

4:38 Sociology is the study of people who do not need to be studied by people who do.

E.S. Turner

4:39 When a woman becomes a scholar there is usually something wrong with her sexual organs.

Friedrich Nietzsche

4:40 There he goes – the man what learned me English.

J.B. Keane

4:41 Those who can – do. Those who cannot – teach. Those who cannot teach become deans.

Thomas L. Martin

4:42 You don't appreciate a lot of stuff in school until you get older. Little things like being spanked every day by a middle-aged woman – stuff you pay good money for in later life.

Emo Philips

4:43 I know you believe you understand what you think I said. But I am not sure you realise that what you heard is not what I meant.

Patrick Murray

29

4:44   As a major shareholder in a laxative company, I demand the abolition of examinations.

Patrick Murray

4:45   If you think education is expensive, try ignorance.

Derek Bok

4:46   Of course I know that 'knickers' begins with a 'k'. I've been to Oxford – it's one of the first things they teach you.

Alan Bennett

4:47   I understand that Harvard University is making its diplomas larger or smaller. I have forgotten which. This is a step in the right direction.

R.M. Hutchins

4:48   The only educational aspect of television is that it puts the repairman's kids through college.

Joan Welsh

4:49   The full area of ignorance is not mapped; we are at present only exploring its fringes.

J.D. Bernal

4:50   When one day they opened a Catholic chapel, which was quickly followed by a pub, a block of shops and eventually a school. The school went up last because there was no profit in it.

Dominic Behan

4:51   When Scythrop grew up, he was sent, as usual, to a public school, where a little learning was painfully beaten into him, and from thence to the university, where it was carefully taken out of him; and he was sent home like a well-threshed ear of corn, with nothing in his head.

Thomas L. Peacock

4:52   It is when the gods hate a man with uncommon abhorrence that they drive him into the profession of a schoolmaster.

Seneca

4:53   I was educated during the holidays from Eton.

Osbert Sitwell

4:54   One can always tell it is summer when one sees school-teachers hanging about the streets idly, looking like canni-bals during a shortage of missionaries.

Robertson Davies

4:55   Teachers are overworked and underpaid. True, it is an exacting and exhausting business, this damming up the flood of human potentialities.

George B. Leonard

4:56   I won't say ours was a tough school, but we had our own coroner. We used to write essays like 'What I'm going to be if I grow up'.

Lenny Bruce

4:57   In our school you were searched for guns and knives on the way in and if you didn't have any, they gave you some.

Emo Philips

4:58   There is nothing on earth intended for innocent people, so horrible as a school. It is in some respects more cruel than a prison. In a prison for example, you are not forced to read books written by the warders and the governor.

George Bernard Shaw

4:59   The Royal Society is a collection of men who elect each other to office and then dine together at the expense of the society to praise each other over wine and award each other medals.

Charles Babbage

4:60   In school we had a name for guys trying to get in touch with themselves.

P.J. O'Rourke

4:61   Like so many ageing college people, Pnin had long ceased to notice the existence of students on the campus.

Vladimir Nabokov

4:62   Education is the inculcation of the incomprehensible into the ignorant by the incompetent.

Josiah Stamp

4:63   I never lecture; not because I am shy or a bad speaker, but simply because I detest the sort of people who go to lectures and don't want to meet them.

H.L. Mencken

4:64   After spending four years as a college star he was a failure at pro football. All he had to show for it was an education.

Patrick Murray

31

4:65   In its fifty years of existence, all the Irish Institute for Advanced Studies has done is to show that there were two Saint Patricks and no God.

Patrick Murray

4:66   But, good gracious, you've got to educate him first. You can't expect a boy to be vicious till he's been to a good school.

H.H. Munro

4:67   I owe a lot to my teachers and mean to pay them back some day.

Stephen Leacock

4:68   When a teacher calls a boy by his entire name it means trouble.

Mark Twain

4:69   My father wanted me to have all the educational opportunities he never had, so he sent me to a girl's school.

Jack Herbert

Food

5:1   We lived for days on nothing but food and water.

W.C. Fields

5:2   Cucumber should be well sliced, dressed with pepper and vinegar, and then thrown out.

Samuel Johnson

5:3   If a lump of soot falls into the soup, and you cannot conveniently get it out, stir it well in, and it will give the soup a French taste.

Jonathan Swift

5:4.   The cook was a good cook, as cooks go; and as cooks go, she went.

H.H. Munro

5:5   Cursed is he that uses peanuts when the recipe calls for almonds.

Christopher Driver

5:6   The secret of staying young is to live honestly, eat slowly and lie about your age.

Lucille Ball

5:7   Two sharks met and one said to the other 'My dear, I've discovered the most wonderful Italian restaurant. It's called the Andrea Doria'.

John Hollander

5:8   Eat at this restaurant and you'll never eat anywhere else again!

Bob Phillips

5:9   House-warming at Zola's – a very tasty dinner, including some grouse whose scented flesh Daudet compared to an old courtesan's flesh marinated in a bidet.

Edmond De Goncourt

5:10   I personally stay away from natural foods. At my age I need all the preservatives I can get.

George Burns

5:11   Americans will eat garbage provided you sprinkle it liberally with ketchup.

Henry Miller

5:12   Not alone is it quite acceptable to breastfeed in a restaurant, but it comes in quite handy when the waiter is late with the cream.

Blanche Knott

5:13   No one goes to that restaurant anymore – it's too crowded.
Yogi Berra

5:14   Whenever cannibals are on the brink of starvation, Heaven, in its infinite mercy, sends them a fat missionary.

Oscar Wilde

5:15   I'm at the age when food has taken the place of sex in my life. In fact, I've just had a mirror put over my kitchen table.
Rodney Dangerfield

5:16   I refuse to spend my life worrying about what I eat. There is no pleasure worth foregoing just for an extra three years in the geriatric ward.

John Mortimer

5:17   The most remarkable thing about my mother is that for thirty years she served the family nothing but leftovers. The original meal has never been found.

Calvin Trillin

5:18   I'm on a grapefruit diet. I eat everything except grapefruit.
Chi Chi Rodriguez

5:19   Is Elizabeth Taylor fat? Her favourite food is seconds.
Joan Rivers

5:20   Our trouble is that we drink too much tea. I see in this the slow revenge of the Orient, which has diverted the Yellow River down our throats.

J.B. Priestley

5:21   Ice-cream is exquisite – what a pity it isn't illegal.
Voltaire

5:22   Eat your vegetables and then you can have your dessert.
Laurence J. Peter

5:23   MacDonald's in Tokyo is a terrible revenge for Pearl Harbour.

S.I. Hayakawa

5:24   A gourmet who thinks of calories is like a tart who looks at her watch.

James Beard

5:25   Only Irish coffee provides in a single glass all four essential food groups: alcohol, caffeine, sugar and fat.

Alex Levine

5:26   Coffee in England always tastes like a chemistry experiment.
Agatha Christie

5:27   Tell the cook of this restaurant with my compliments that these are the very worst sandwiches in the whole world, and that, when I ask for a watercress sandwich, I do not mean a loaf with a field in the middle of it.

Oscar Wilde

5:28   I often take exercise. Why only yesterday I had breakfast in bed.

Oscar Wilde

5:29   I am not a vegetarian because I love animals; I'm a vegetarian because I hate plants.

A. W. Brown

5:30   To duplicate the taste of hammer-head shark, boil old newspapers in Sloan's Liniment.

Spike Milligan

5:31   For the chicken the egg demands involvement but for the pig bacon demands total commitment.

John A. Price

5:32   Hotel tea is when you have to mix together a plastic envelope containing too much sugar, a small plastic pot of something which is not milk but has curdled anyway, and a thin brown packet seemingly containing the ashes of a cremated mole.

Frank Muir

5:33   If you are ever at a loss to support a flagging conversation, introduce the subject of eating.

Leigh Hunt

5:34   Wearers of a Balliol tie enjoy a traditional immunity from
       cannibalism.

                                                              Lord Elton

5:35   In marital conflicts nothing should be thrown that is bigger
       than a bread box. Pie throwing is out of the question because
       if you bake like I do, a direct hit with one of those things
       could kill you.

                                                          Phyllis Diller

5:36   I have just given up spinach for Lent.

                                                    F. Scott Fitzgerald

5:37   It is odd how all men develop the notion, as they grow older,
       that their mothers were wonderful cooks. I have yet to meet
       a man who will admit that his mother was a kitchen assassin
       and nearly poisoned him.

                                                        Robertson Davies

5:38   I bought all those Jane Fonda videos. I love to sit and eat
       cookies and watch them.

                                                            Dolly Parton

5:39   I just love Chinese food. My favourite dish is number 27.
                                                           Clement Atlee

5:40   I could never learn to like her – except on a raft at sea with
       no other provisions in sight.

                                                             Mark Twain

5:41   The first law of dietetics seems to be: if it tastes good, it's bad
       for you.

                                                            Isaac Asimov

5:42   The worst thing that ever happened me was that I offered a
       fellow a crisp from my bag and he took two.

                                                             Vic Reeves

5:43   My wife does wonderful things with leftovers. She throws
       them out.

                                                            Herb Shriner

5:44   A food is not necessarily essential just beause your child
       hates it.

                                                    Katharine Whitehorn

5:45 Food is an important part of a balanced diet.

Fran Lebowitz

5:46 Some breakfast food manufacturer hit upon the simple notion of emptying out the leavings of carthorse nosebags, adding a few other things like unconsumed portions of chicken layers mash, and the sweepings of racing stables, packing the mixture in little bags and selling them in health food shops.

Frank Muir

5:47 Nouvelle cuisine, roughly translated, means 'I can't believe I spent ninety-six dollars and I'm still hungry.'

Mike Kalin

5:48 Another good reducing exercise consists in placing both hands against the table edge and pushing back.

Robert Quillen

Lawyers and other Professions

6:1   The first thing we do, let's kill all lawyers.
William Shakespeare

6:2   An actuary is someone who cannot stand the excitement of chartered accountancy.
Glan Thomas

6:3   Justice must not only be done, it must be seen to be believed.
J.B. Morton

6:4   I have nothing against undertakers personally. It's just that I wouldn't want one to bury my sister.
Jessica Mitford

6:5   Only lawyers and mental defectives are automatically exempt from jury duty.
George Bernard Shaw

6:6   When I came back to Dublin I was courtmartialed in my absence and sentenced to death in my absence, so I said they could shoot me in my absence.
Brendan Behan

6:7   It's not the people who are in prison that worry me. It's the people who aren't.
Arthur Gore

6:8   A person guilty of rape should be castrated. That would stop him pretty quick.
Billy Graham

6:9   No brilliance is required in the law, just common sense and relatively clean fingernails.
John Mortimer

6:10   The thrill of hearing a jury return a guilty verdict is the ultimate sexual experience.
Judge Gregory Wallance

6:11   I am on record as saying that Simon Cameron would not steal a red-hot stove. I now wish to withdraw that statement.

Thaddeus Stevens

6:12   A lawyer is a learned gentleman who rescues your estate from your enemies and keeps it to himself.

Henry Brougham

6:13   Probably the only place where a man can feel really secure is in a maximum security prison, except for the imminent threat of release.

Germaine Greer

6:14   The court was not previously aware of the prisoner's many accomplishments. In view of these, we see fit to impose the death penalty.

Quentin Crisp

6:15   I went to see him hanged, drawn, and quartered, which was done, he looking as cheerful as any man could do in that condition.

Samuel Pepys

6:16   The only difference between doctors and lawyers is that lawyers merely rob you, whereas doctors rob you and kill you, too.

Anton Chekhov

6:17   Curiosity killed the cat, but for a while I was a suspect.

Steven Wright

6:18   There are three reasons why lawyers are replacing rats as laboratory research animals. One is that they are plentiful, another is that the lab assistants don't get so attached to them and the third is that they will do things you just can't get rats to do.

Blanche Knott

6:19   My barber is an authority on everything except how to cut hair properly.

William H. Roylance

6:20   If once a man indulges himself in murder, very soon he comes to think very little of robbing; and from robbing he comes next to drinking and whistling on the Sabbath, and from that to incivility and procrastination. Once you begin upon this downward path you never know where you are to stop. Many a man has dated his ruin from some murder or other that perhaps he thought little of at that time.

Thomas De Quincey

6:21   Where there is no patrol car, there is no speed limit.

Petr Beckmann

6:22   A countryman between two lawyers is like a fish between two cats.

Benjamin Franklin

6:23   As repressed sadists are supposed to become policemen or butchers, so those with an irrational fear of life become publishers.

Cyril Connolly

6:24   If capital punishment was good enough for my father, it's good enough for me.

Victor Moore

6:25   A lawyer will do anything to win a case. Sometimes, he will even tell the truth.

Patrick Murray

6:26   The penalty for laughing in a courtroom is six months in jail – if it weren't for this penalty, the jury would never hear the evidence.

Bob Hope

6:27   I believe capital punishment to be an appropriate remedy for anyone who does me injury, but under no other circumstances.

F.L. Bailey

6:28   As one solicitor once wrote to another, 'Sir, I regret to inform you that there is danger of agreement breaking out between our respective clients'.

Reginald Hine

6:29   Death is not the end. There remains the litigation over the estate.

Ambrose Bierce

6:30   After a year in therapy, my psychiatrist said to me, 'Maybe life isn't for everyone'.

Larry Brown

6:31   Only one thing is impossible for God – to find any sense in any copyright law on the planet.

Mark Twain

6:32   The Scottish verdict 'not proven' means 'guilty, but don't do it again'.

Winifred Duke

6:33   An expert is one who knows so much about so little that he neither can be contradicted, nor is worth contradicting.

Henry Ward

6:34   You can discourage burglars by wearing an old policeman's uniform and standing outside your house all day and night.

G. Byker

6:35   Why are there 12 jurors? Because there are 12 tribes of Israel, 12 months in a year, 12 inches in a foot, and 12 apostles.

Quentin Hogg

6:36   The right to pay fees to lawyers is a fundamental and ancient human right, and is at the kernel of what we know as democracy.

Flann O'Brien

6:37   1974 was the last time that Al Davis and I spoke without lawyers being paid.

Gene Klein

6:38   My definition of utter waste is a coachload of lawyers going over a cliff with three empty seats.

Lamar Hunt

6:39   Players like rules. If they didn't have any rules, they wouldn't have anything to break.

Lee Walls

6:40   I don't want a lawyer to tell me what I cannot do; I hire him to tell me how to do what I want to do.

J.P. Morgan

6:41   The most beautiful words in the English language are 'not guilty'.

Maxim Gorky

Literature

7:1   I never read a book before reviewing it. I find that it just prejudices me.

Sydney Smith

7:2   Read over your compositions, and wherever you meet with a passage which you think is particularly fine, strike it out.

Samuel Johnson

7:3   The dawn is a term for the early morning used by poets and other people who don't have to get up.

Oliver Herford

7:4   He has produced a couplet. When our friend is delivered of a couplet, with infinite labour and pain, he takes to his bed, has straw laid down, the knocker tied up, and expects his friends to call and make enquiries.

Sydney Smith

7:5   Two people getting together to write a book is like three people getting together to have a baby. One of them is superfluous.

George Bernard Shaw

7:6   I never travel without my diary. One should always have something sensational to read in the train.

Oscar Wilde

7:7   My only claim to literary fame is that I used to deliver meat to a woman who became T. S. Eliot's mother-in-law.

Alan Bennett

7:8   If you want to get rich from writing, write the sort of thing that's read by persons who move their lips when they're reading to themselves.

Don Marquis

7:9   You may certainly not kiss the hand that wrote *Ulysses*. It's done lots of other things as well.

James Joyce

7:10   An editor should have a pimp for a brother so he can have someone to look up to.

Gene Fowler

7:11   Your manuscript is both good and original; but the part that is good is not original, and the part that is original is not good.

Samuel Johnson

7:12   Immature poets imitate; mature poets steal.

T.S. Eliot

7:13   This is not a book to be tossed aside lightly. It should be thrown with great force.

Dorothy Parker

7:14   I am sitting in the smallest room in the house. I have your review before me. It will soon be behind me.

Max Reger

7:15   I have been told by hospital authorities that more copies of my works are left behind by departing patients than those of any other author.

Robert Benchley

7:16   George Bernard Shaw writes like a Pakistani who has learned English when he was twelve years old to become a chartered accountant.

John Osborne

7:17   The Poems of Seth will be remembered long after those of Homer and Virgil are forgotten – but not until then.

Richard Porson

7:18   Reading Proust is like bathing in someone else's dirty water.

Alexander Woollcott

7:19   Finishing a book is just like you took a child out in the yard and shot it.

Truman Capote

7:20   For those who like this sort of thing, this is the sort of thing they will like.

Max Beerbohm

7:21   Donne's verses are like the peace and mercy of God. Like His peace, they pass all understanding, and like His mercy they seem to endure forever.

King James I

7:22   I was working on the proofs of one of my poems all day. In the morning I put a comma in and in the afternoon I took it back out again.

Oscar Wilde

7:23   Originality is undetected plagiarism.

W.R. Ince

7:24   Free verse is like playing tennis with the net down.

Robert Frost

7:25   I have read only one book in my life, and that is *White Fang*. It's so frightfully good I've never bothered to read another.

Nancy Mitford

7:26   There are two ways of disliking poetry. One way is to dislike it, and the other is to read Pope.

Oscar Wilde

7:27   Many thanks for your book – I shall lose no time in reading it.

Benjamin Disraeli

7:28   Warren Harding, the only man, woman, or child who ever wrote a simple declarative sentence with seven grammatical errors, is dead.

e.e. Cummings

7:29   To me Poe's prose is unreadable – like Jane Austen's. No, there is a difference. I could read Poe's prose on a salary, but not Jane Austen's.

Mark Twain

7:30   Mr Irvin Cobb took me into his library and showed me his books, of which he has a complete set.

Ring Lardner

7:31   Mr Waugh is a parochial English writer (tautologies gush from my pen!)

Gore Vidal

7:32   Writers of thrillers tend to gravitate to the Secret Service as the mentally unstable become psychiatrists and the impotent become pornographers.

Malcolm Muggeridge

7:33   On the day when a young writer corrects his first proof sheets, he is as proud as a schoolboy who has just got his first dose of pox.

Charles Baudelaire

7:34   His books are going like wildfire – everybody is burning them.

George De Witt

7:35   I am addicted to literature. I never go anywhere without a Trollope.

Alec Guinness

7:36   Your function as a critic is to show that it is really you yourself who should have written the book, if you had had the time, and since you hadn't you are glad that someone else had, although obviously it might have been done better.

Stephen Potter

7:37   Shakespeare said pretty well everything and what he left out, James Joyce, with a nudge from meself, put in.

Brendan Behan

7:38   When I want to read a book, I write one.

Benjamin Disraeli

7:39   *Paradise Lost* is a book that, once put down, is very hard to pick up again.

Samuel Johnson

7:40   Oscar Wilde paraphrased and inverted the witticisms and epigrams of others. His method of literary piracy was on the lines of the robber Cacus, who dragged stolen cows backwards by the tails to his cavern so that their hoofprints might not lead to detection.

George Moore

7:41   This book of Italian literature shows a want of knowledge that must be the result of years of study.

Oscar Wilde

7:42   If you steal from one author, it's plagiarism; if you steal from many, it's research.

Wilson Mizner

7:43   I've given up reading books. I find it takes my mind off myself.

Oscar Wilde

7:44   Jeffrey Archer is proof of the proposition that in each of us there lurks a bad novel.

Julian Critchley

7:45   He was an author whose works were so little known as to be almost confidential.

Stanley Walker

7:46   There are just three rules for writing – but nobody knows what they are.

Somerset Maugham

7:47   G.K. Chesterton and Hilaire Belloc were the two buttocks of one bum.

T. Sturge Moore

7:48   This book is dedicated to the one woman fate created just for me. So far I've managed to avoid her.

Jon Winokur

7:49   Thomas Gray walks as if he had fouled his small-clothes, and looks as if he smelt it.

Christopher Smart

7:50   Perhaps the saddest lot that can befall mortal man is to be the husband of a lady poet.

George Jean Nathan

7:51   George Sand was a great cow-full of ink.

Gustave Flaubert

7:52   My brother-in-law wrote an unusual murder story. The victim got killed by a man from another book.

Robert Sylvester

7:53   Nobody ever went broke underestimating the taste of the American public.

H.L. Mencken

7:54 It is wrong to lecture on a living poet. One performs autopsies only on corpses.

Robert Graves

7:55 I always read the last page of a book first so that if I die before I finish I'll know how it turned out.

Nora Ephron

7:56 A publisher would as soon see a burglar in his office as a poet.

H. De Vere Stacpoole

7:57 Most of today's books have an air of having been written in one day from books read the night before.

N.S. Chamfort

7:58 If you can't annoy somebody there is little point in writing.

Kinglsey Amis

7:59 God created the poet, then took a handful of the rubbish that was left and made three critics.

T.J. Thomas

7:60 When in doubt, ascribe all quotations to George Bernard Shaw.

Nigel Rees

7:61 Nature, not content with denying him the art of thinking, conferred on him the gift of writing.

George Bernard Shaw

7:62 James, why don't you write books that people can read?

Nora Joyce

7:63 Before they made S.J. Perelman they broke the mould.

Groucho Marx

7:64 The censorious said that she slept in a hammock and understood Yeats's poems but her family denied both stories.

H.H. Munro

7:65 It is a mean thief or a successful author who plunders the dead.

Austin O'Malley

7:66   Waldo is one of those people who would be enormously
        improved by death.

                                                H.H. Munro

7:67   Shaw is the spinster aunt of English literature.

                                                Kenneth Tynan

7:68   The author of this novel and all the characters mentioned in
        it are fictitious. There is no such city as Manchester.

                                                Howard Spring

7:69   Concerning no subject would Shaw be deterred by the minor
        accident of total ignorance from penning a definitive
        opinion.

                                                Roger Scruton

7:70   She is so unreadable that people will finally believe her to be
        a classic.

                                                Ernest Hemingway

7:71   This is the sixth book I've written, which isn't bad for a guy
        who has only read two.

                                                George Burns

7:72   Every word that Lillian Hellman writes is a lie, including
        'and' and 'the'.

                                                Mary McCarthy

7:73   I can forgive Alfred Nobel for having invented dynamite,
        but only a fiend in human form could have invented the
        Nobel Prize.

                                                George Bernard Shaw

7:74   There is no greater bliss in life than when the plumber
        eventually comes to unblock your drains. No writer can give
        that sort of pleasure.

                                                Victoria Glendinning

7:75   It took twelve years to undo the harm caused by Housman's
        lecture on poetry.

                                                I.A. Richards

7:76   Robert Bridges's anthology, *The Spirit of Man*, is like a vomit
        after a rich meal.

                                                A.C. Benson

7:77 Mr C.L. Dodgson neither claims nor acknowledges any connection with any pseudonym or with any book not published under his own name.

Lewis Carroll

7:78 I did so enjoy your book darling. Everything that everybody writes in it is so good.

Mrs Patrick Campbell

7:79 I would cheerfully pay George Bernard Shaw's funeral expenses at any time.

Henry Irving

7:80 In Ireland they try to make a cat clean by rubbing its nose in its own filth. James Joyce has tried the same treatment on the human subject. I hope it may prove successful.

George Bernard Shaw

7:81 We all know of course that women are habitually constipated, but to represent them in fiction as being altogether devoid of a back passage seems to me really an excess of chivalry.

Somerset Maugham

7:82 The preface is the most important part of a book. Even reviewers read a preface.

Philip Guedalla

7:83 A woman who writes commits two sins; she increases the number of books and decreases the number of women.

Alphonse Kerr

7:84 If we cannot stamp out literature in our own country, we can at least stop it being brought in from outside.

Evelyn Waugh

7:85 It was a book to kill time for those who like it better dead.

Rose MacAulay

7:86 I often quote myself. It adds spice to my conversation.

George Bernard Shaw

7:87 Now that I know I am about to die, all right then, I'll say it: Dante makes me sick.

L.F. De Vega-Carpio

7:88   One should not be too severe on English novels; they are the only relaxation of the intellectually unemployed.

Oscar Wilde

7:89   Writing is easy. All you have to do is to stare at a blank piece of paper until drops of blood form on your forehead.

Gene Fowler

7:90   If a third of all the novelists and maybe two-thirds of all the poets now writing dropped dead suddenly, the loss to literature would not be great.

Charles Osborne

7:91   Magazines all too frequently lead to books and should be regarded as the heavy petting of literature.

Fran Lebowitz

7:92   First coffee. Then a bowel movement. Then the muse joins me.

Gore Vidal

7:93   I thought I'd begin by reading a poem by Shakespeare, but then I thought 'why should I?' He never reads any of mine.

Spike Milligan

7:94   I am not feeling very well. I can only write prose today.

W.B. Yeats

7:95   The most important difference between poetry and any other branch of publishing is, that whereas with most categories of books you are aiming to make as much money as possible, with poetry you are aiming to lose as little as possible.

T.S. Eliot

7:96   *Andiatorocte* is the title of a volume of poems by the Rev. Clarence Walworth, of Albany N.Y. It is a word borrowed from the Indians, and should, we think, be returned to them as soon as possible.

Oscar Wilde

7:97   This erratum slip has been inserted by mistake.

Alisdair Gray

7:98   In America only the successful writer is important, in France all writers are important, in England no writer is important, and in Australia you have to explain what a writer is.

Geoffrey Cotterell

7:99   A good many young writers make the mistake of enclosing a stamped self-addressed envelope, big enough to send the manuscript back in. This is too much of a temptation for the editor.

Ring Lardner

7:100 Studying literature at Harvard is like learning about women at the Mayo Clinic.

Roy Blount

7:101 If a writer has to rob his mother, he will not hesitate; 'Ode to a Grecian Urn' is worth any number of old ladies.

William Faulkner

7:102 If I should die, think only this of me
       That in some corner of a foreign field
       There lies a plagiarist.

Derek Alder

7:103 He is a distinguished man of letters. He works for the Post Office.

Max Kaufmann

Living – Family and Relations

8:1   If you don't clean your house for two months it doesn't get any dirtier.

Quentin Crisp

8:2   Never go to bed mad – stay up and fight.

Phyllis Diller

8:3   The General was essentially a man of peace – except of course in his domestic affairs.

Oscar Wilde

8:4   Insanity is hereditary; you can get it from your children.

Sam Levenson

8:5   I love children. Especially when they cry – for then someone takes them away.

Nancy Mitford

8:6   It's better to be black than gay because when you're black you don't have to tell your mother.

Charles Pierce

8:7   Every time a child says 'I don't believe in fairies', there's a little fairy somewhere that falls down dead.

J.M. Barrie

8:8   Why should we do anything for posterity? What has posterity ever done for us?

Joseph Addison

8:9   Children really brighten up a household – they never turn the lights off.

Ralph Bus

8:10 I have never understood this liking for war. It panders to instincts already well catered for within the scope of any respectable domestic establishment.

Alan Bennett

8:11   Any astronomer can predict with absolute accuracy just where every star in the universe will be at 11.30 tonight. He can make no such prediction about his teenage daughter.
James T. Adams

8:12   Watching your daughter being collected by her date feels like handing over a million dollar Stradivarius to a gorilla.
Jim Bishop

8:13   My husband and I have decided to start a family while my parents are still young enough to look after them.
Rita Rudner

8:14   You cannot be happy with a woman who pronounces the first 'd' in Wednesday.
Peter De Vries

8:15   When I go to the beauty parlour, I always use the emergency entrance. Sometimes I just go for an estimate.
Phyllis Diller

8:16   Most women are not as young as they are painted.
Max Beerbohm

8:17   My aunt once sent me a postal order for five pounds for coming top of a list.
F.W. Abernathy

8:18   Have you ever had one of those days when you have had to murder a loved one because he is the devil?
Emo Philips

8:19   Another good thing about being poor is that when you are seventy your children will not have you declared legally insane in order to gain control of your estate.
Woody Allen

8:20   Your mother, sir, under the pretence of keeping a bawdy house, was in reality a receiver of stolen property.
Samuel Johnson

8:21   Some mornings it just doesn't seem worth it to gnaw through the leather straps.
Emo Philips

8:22 There are three stages of man: he believes in Santa Claus; he does not believe in Santa Claus; he is Santa Claus.

Bob Phillips

8:23 To watch a child drowning within a few yards of me has a dispiriting effect upon my appetite.

Harry Graham

8:24 The child was a keen bed-wetter.

Noel Coward

8:25 She invariably was first over the fence in the mad pursuit of culture.

George Ade

8:26 I never met a kid I liked.

W.C. Fields

8:27 Few misfortunes can befall a boy which bring worse consequences than to have a really affectionate mother.

Somerset Maugham

8:28 Anyone who hates children and animals can't be all bad.

W.C. Fields

8:29 I have good looking kids; thank goodness my wife cheats on me.

Rodney Dangerfield

8:30 The flashier kind of widow may insist on sleeping with only black men during the first year after the death.

P.J. O'Rourke

8:31 My folks first met on the subway trying to pick each other's pockets.

Freddie Prinze

8:32 I cannot tell you if genius is hereditary, because heaven has granted me no offspring.

James McNeill Whistler

8:33 He is like a mule, with neither pride of ancestry nor hope of posterity.

Robert G. Ingersoll

8:34   Whatever women do they must do twice as well as men to be thought half as good. Luckily, this is not difficult.

Charlotte Whitton

8:35   Even if your father had spent more of your mother's immoral earnings on your education you would still not be a gentleman.

Frank Otter

8:36   Last week I stated that this woman was the ugliest woman I had ever seen. I have since been visited by her sister and now wish to withdraw that statement.

Mark Twain

8:37   The best way to find something you have lost is to buy a replacement.

Ann Landers

8:38   I hate housework! You make the beds, you do the dishes – and six months later you have to start all over again.

Joan Rivers

8:39   There are three ages of man – youth, age, and 'you're looking wonderful'.

Francis Spellman

8:40   In general my children refuse to eat anything that hasn't danced on television.

Erma Bombeck

8:41   An extravagance is anything you buy that is of no earthly use to your wife.

Franklin P. Adams

8:42   Children nowadays are tyrants. They contradict their parents, gobble their food, and tyrannise their teachers.

Socrates (425 B.C.)

8:43   A genius is a man who can rewrap a new shirt and not have any pins left over.

Dino Levi

8:44   It was very good of God to let Thomas and Mrs Carlyle marry one another and so make only two people miserable instead of four.

Samuel Butler

8:45   Wealth is any income that is at least one hundred dollars a year more than the income of one's wife's sister's husband.

H.L. Mencken

8:46   All a child can expect is that its father be present at the conception.

Joe Orton

8:47   Having a family is like having a bowling alley installed in your head.

Martin Mull

8:48   I like children – fried.

W.C. Fields

8:49   There are only two things that a child will share willingly – communicable diseases and its mother's age.

Benjamin Spock

8:50   Man is not born free, he is attached to his mother by a cord and is not capable of looking after himself for at least seven years (seventy in some cases).

Katharine Whitehorn

8:51   I was much distressed by the next door people who had twin babies and played the violin; but one of the twins has died, and the other has eaten the fiddle – so all is peace.

Edward Lear

8:52   The baby is fine. The only problem is that he looks like Edward G. Robinson.

Woody Allen

8:53   My wife has a slight impediment in her speech – every now and then she stops to breathe.

Jimmy Durante

8:54   I have never got over the embarrassing fact that I was born in bed with a woman.

Wilson Mizner

8:55   She was one of those women who go through life demanding to see the manager.

G. Patrick

8:56   When you see a married couple coming down the street, the one who is two or three steps ahead is the one that's mad.

Helen Rowland

8:57   A lot of people would rather tour sewers than visit their cousins.

Jane Howard

8:58   I love mankind – it's people I can't stand.

Charles Schultz

8:59   Childhood is that wonderful time of life when all you need to do to lose weight is to take a bath.

Richard S. Zera

8:60   Alimony is like buying oats for a dead horse.

Louis A. Safian

8:61   To lose one parent may be regarded as a misfortune; to lose both looks like carelessness.

Oscar Wilde

8:62   The ultimate penalty for bigamy is two mothers-in-law.

George Russell

8:63   Retirement at sixty-five is ridiculous. When I was sixty-five I still had pimples.

George Burns

8:64   Leon Britten looked like a bloke in the sixth form who never had a date.

Simon Hoggart

8:65   I don't feel old – I don't feel anything until noon. Then it's time for my nap.

Bob Hope

8:66   When I was a boy, the Dead Sea was only sick.

George Burns

8:67   Why a four year old child could understand this report. Run out and find me a four year old child. I can't make head nor tail out of it.

Groucho Marx

8:68   Every day, in every way, I get worse and worse.

Patrick Murray

8:69   He was watching the moon come up lazily out of the old
       cemetery in which nine of his daughters were lying, and
       only two of whom were dead.

James Thurber

8:70   Santa Claus has the right idea – visit people only once a year.

Victor Borge

8:71   Isn't it funny how everyone in favour of abortion has
       already been born?

Patrick Murray

8:72   No man who has wrestled with a self-adjusting card table
       can ever be quite the man he once was.

James Thurber

8:73   The main difference between an Essex girl and a super-
       market trolley is that a supermarket trolley has a mind of its
       own.

Ray Leigh

8:74   I know I was cruel to other children because I remember
       stuffing their nostrils with putty, and beating a little boy
       with stinging nettles.

Vita Sackville-West

8:75   The real menace in dealing with a five year old is that in no
       time at all you begin to sound like a five year old.

Jean Kerr

8:76   When Lady Louise Moncrieff's sixteenth child was born, her
       sister was present and called out 'It's all right Louise, and
       you have got another little boy'. And the reply of the poor
       tired lady was 'My dear, I really don't care if it is a parrot'.

Lord Ormathwaite

8:77   I love to go to the playground and watch the children
       jumping up and down. They don't know I'm firing blanks.

Emo Philips

8:78   The male is a domestic animal which, if treated with firm-
       ness and kindness, can be trained to do most things.

Jilly Cooper

8:79   I'd love to slit my mother-in-law's corsets and watch her
       spread to death.

Phyllis Diller

8:80 You know you're getting old when you stoop to tie your shoes and wonder what else you can do while you're down there.

George Burns

8:81 I was the kid next door's imaginary friend.

Emo Philips

8:82 I am the only woman in the world who has her dresses rejected by the Salvation Army.

Phyllis Diller

8:83 The highlight of my childhood was making my brother laugh so hard the food came out of his nose.

Garrison Keillor

8:84 The worst sensation I know of is getting up at night and stepping on a toy train.

Kin Hubbard

8:85 My grandfather started walking five miles a day when he was sixty. Now he's eighty-five and we don't know where the hell he is.

Ellen De Generis

8:86 Two can live as cheaply as one, but it costs them twice as much.

Frank Sullivan

8:87 My parents warned me never to open the cellar door or I would see things I shouldn't see. So one day when they were out I did open the cellar door and I did see things I shouldn't see – grass, flowers, the sun ...

Emo Philips

8:88 Tell your nice mummies and daddies to buy this book for you and hit them until they do.

Spike Milligan

8:89 Distant relatives are the best kind and the further away the better.

Kin Hubbard

8:90 When you see what some girls marry, you realise how they must hate to work for a living.

Helen Rowland

8:91   I do wish I could tell you my age, but it is impossible. It keeps changing all the time.

Greer Garson

8:92   Children are the most desirable opponents at Scrabble as they are both easy to beat and fun to cheat.

Fran Lebowitz

8:93   The trouble with children is that they are not returnable.

Quentin Crisp

8:94   I took my mother-in-law to Madam Tussaud's Chamber of Horrors and one of the attendants said 'Keep her moving sir, we're stocktaking'.

Les Dawson

8:95   I'm at that age now where just putting my cigar in its holder is a thrill.

George Burns

8:96   One of the delights known to age and beyond the grasp of youth is that of *not going*.

J.B. Priestley

8:97   The one phrase it is imperative to know in every foreign language is 'my friend will pay'.

Alan Whicker

8:98   I've never struck a woman in my life – not even my own mother.

W.C. Fields

8:99   I cannot believe that out of 100,000 sperm, you were the quickest.

Steven Pearl

8:100   Reinhart was never his mother's favourite – and he was an only child.

Thomas Berger

8:101   Wild horses couldn't drag a secret out of most women. However, women seldom have lunch with wild horses.

Ivern Boyett

8:102   When a woman says, 'I don't wish to mention any names', it ain't necessary to mention any names.

Kin Hubbard

8:103 A Boy Scout troop is a lot of boys dressed as jerks, led by a jerk dressed as a boy.

Shelley Berman

8:104 Nowadays, they spend £10,000 for a school bus to pick the kids right up at the door so they don't have to walk. Then they spend £200,000 for a gym so they can get some exercise.

Red Blanchard

8:105 I'm very pleased to be here. Let's face it, at my age I'm very pleased to be anywhere.

George Burns

8:106 My mother didn't breastfeed me. She said she just liked me as a friend.

Rodney Dangerfield

8:107 Help a man in trouble and he'll never forget you – especially the next time he's in trouble.

Johnny Lyons

8:108 I have already given two cousins to the war and I am ready to sacrifice my wife's brother.

Artemus Ward

8:109 What ought to be done to the man who invented the celebrating of anniversaries? Mere killing would be too light.

Mark Twain

8:110 I have had more trouble with D.L. Moody than with any other man I ever met.

D.L. Moody

8:111 The woman who can sacrifice a clean unspoiled penny stamp is probably unborn.

H.H. Munro

8:112 Mother Nature is wonderful. She gives us twelve years to develop a love for our children before turning them into teenagers.

Eugene P. Bertin

8:113 I understand the importance of bondage between parent and child.

Dan Quayle

8:114 Friends are people who borrow books and set wet glasses on them.

E.A. Robinson

8:115 They say such nice things about people at their funerals that it makes me sad to realise that I'm going to miss mine by just a few days.

Garrison Keillor

8:116 Fraser left his children unbaptised – but his wife did it secretly in the washing basin.

Virginia Woolf

8:117 As Miss America, my goal is to bring peace to the entire world and then get my own apartment.

Jay Leno

8:118 Take a small boy smeared with honey and lower him between the walls. The bees will fasten themselves to him by the hundreds and can be scraped off when he is pulled up, after which the boy can be thrown away. If no small boy smeared with honey can be found, it may be necessary to take an ordinary small boy and smear him, which should be a pleasure.

S.J. Perelman

8:119 As he was lowering the body into its last resting place, the respected grave-digger suddenly collapsed and died, which event cast a gloom over the entire proceedings.

Bernard Falck

8:120 It takes forty dumb animals to make a fur coat, but only one to wear it.

Bryn Jones

8:121 I'm going home next week. It's a kind of emergency – my parents are coming here.

Rita Rudner

8:122 I think that husbands and wives should live in separate houses. If there's enough money, the children should live in a third.

Cloris Leachman

8:123 We never talked in our family. We communicated by putting Ann Landers articles on the fridge.

Judy Gold

8:124 My photographs do me an injustice. They look just like me.
Phyllis Diller

8:125 My grandmother was a very tough woman. She buried three husbands and two of them were just napping.
Rita Rudner

8:126 I have problems flown in fresh daily wherever I am.
Richard Lewis

8:127 People ask me what I'd most appreciate getting for my eighty-seventh birthday. I'll tell you: a paternity suit.
George Burns

8:128 When I was a girl I had only two friends, and they were imaginary. And they would only play with each other.
Rita Rudner

8:129 Until I was thirteen, I thought my name was 'shut up'.
Joe Namath

8:130 Happiness is having a large, loving, caring, close-knit family in another city.
George Burns

8:131 I am thirty years old, but I read at the thirty-four year old level.
Dana Carvey

8:132 When I was a boy of fourteen, my father was so ignorant I could hardly stand to have the old man around. But when I got to be twenty-one, I was astonished at how much he had learned in seven years.
Mark Twain

8:133 When I was a child, I wanted to be an invalid when I grew up.
Quentin Crisp

8:134 I don't plan to grow old gracefully. I plan to have face lifts until my ears meet.
Rita Rudner

8:135 Alimony is the curse of the working classes.
Norman Mailer

8:136 Somewhere on this earth, every ten seconds, a woman gives birth to a child. We must find this woman and stop her at once.

Sam Levenson

8:137 Never lend your car to anyone to whom you have given birth.

Erma Bombeck

8:138 At my age flowers scare me.

George Burns

8:139 Picasso was a delightful, kindly, friendly, simple little man. When I met him he was extremely excited and overjoyed because his mother-in-law had just died and he was looking forward to the funeral.

Edith Sitwell

8:140 Never put off until tomorrow what can be put off until the day after tomorrow just as well.

Mark Twain

8:141 Remember, blood is not only thicker than water, it's much more difficult to get off the carpet.

Phyllis Diller

8:142 My mother was like a sister to me, only we didn't have sex quite so often.

Emo Philips

8:143 One or two days before moving house, place your goldfish bowl in the freezer. When the time comes to move you will find that your fish can be transported in a car or van with no danger of spillage.

D.A. Roberts

8:144 If a man smiles in his own house, somebody is sure to ask him for money.

William Feather

8:145 Once, when somebody in our house stepped on the cat's paw, my mother turned to the cat and said sternly 'I told you not go around barefoot!'

Zero Mostel

8:146　My mother-in-law had to stop skipping for exercise. It registered seven on the Richter Scale.

Les Dawson

8:147　Dahlia is my good and deserving aunt, not to be confused with Aunt Agatha, who eats broken bottles and wears barbed wire next to the skin.

P.G. Wodehouse

8:148　While your mother-in-law is alive, domestic peace is out of the question.

Juvenal

8:149　It is a singular fact that a month or two before his daughter's marriage, the father, the husband, the bread-winner, who has made the whole affair possible, is afflicted with imbecility – that is in the estimation of the female members of the tribe. They fuss and buzz about like a swarm of bees, arranging, planning, arguing, advising, whispering in corners, yelling over the telephone, buying this and ordering that. The only person never consulted, never allowed to open his mouth is Daddy, who 'doesn't understand'.

A.P. Herbert

8:150　There are two things in this life for which we are never fully prepared. Twins.

Josh Billings

8:151　To be a successful father there is one absolute rule: 'when you have a kid, don't look at it for the first two years'.

Ernest Hemingway

8:152　During the blitz I was asked if I wanted to have my books or my son evacuated to the safety of the country. I chose my books because many of them were irreplaceable but I could always have another son.

Evelyn Waugh

8:153　I was born in Lowell, Massachusetts, and the explanation is quite simple. I wished to be near my mother.

James McNeill Whistler

8:154　I am so busy I have had to put off the date of my death.

Bertrand Russell

8:155 I didn't hire Scott as assistant coach because he's my son. I hired him because I'm married to his mother.

Frank Layden

8:156 For the parent of a Little Leaguer, a baseball game is simply a nervous breakdown divided into innings.

Earl Wilson

8:157 I owe a lot to my parents – especially my mother and father.

Greg Norman

8:158 Teenagers, are you tired of being harassed by your stupid parents? Act now. Move out, get a job, and pay your own bills – while you still know everything.

John Hinde

8:159 Adam was the luckiest man in the world – he had no mother-in-law.

Sholom Aleichem

8:160 I have just returned from a children's party. I am one of the survivors. There are not many of us.

Percy French

8:161 There are three ways to get something done; do it yourself, hire someone, or forbid your kids to do it.

Mona Crane

8:162 On the plus side, death is one of the few things that can be done as easily lying down.

Woody Allen

8:163 My uncle Sammy was an angry man. He had printed on his tombstone 'What are you looking at?'

Margaret Smith

8:164 Never raise a hand to your kids. It leaves your groin unprotected.

Red Buttons

8:165 My father never took me to the zoo. He said if they want me they will come and get me.

Rodney Dangerfield

Love, Sex, Marriage, Men and Women

9:1 He said it was artificial respiration, but now I find that I am to have his child.

Anthony Burgess

9:2 Sara could commit adultery at one end and weep for her sins at the other, and enjoy both operations at once.

Joyce Cary

9:3 Sex without love is an empty experience, but as empty experiences go, it's a pretty good empty experience.

Woody Allen

9:4 All this fuss about sleeping together. For physical pleasure I'd sooner go to my dentist any day.

Evelyn Waugh

9:5 It's so long since I've had sex I've forgotten who ties up whom.

Joan Rivers

9:6 The world is full of people who are ready to think the worst when they see a man sneaking out of the wrong bedroom in the middle of the night.

Will Cuppy

9:7 The majority of husbands remind me of an orangutang trying to play the violin.

Honoré De Balzac

9:8 It is well to write love letters. There are certain things it is not easy to ask your mistress for face to face – like money for instance.

Henri De Regnier

9:9 In the circles in which I move, sleeping with a woman does not constitute an introduction.

Virginia McLeod

9:10 I thought men like that shot themselves.

King George V

9:11   The quickest way to a man's heart is through his chest.
Roseanne Barr

9:12   If it wasn't for pickpockets and frisking at airports I wouldn't have any sex life at all.
Rodney Dangerfield

9:13   A lady is a woman who never shows her underwear unintentionally.
Lillian Day

9:14   I'm such a good lover because I practise a lot on my own.
Woody Allen

9:15   A eunuch is a man who has had his works cut out for him.
Robert Byrne

9:16   His designs were strictly honourable; that is to rob a lady of her fortune by way of marriage.
Henry Fielding

9:17   Sex between a man and a woman can be wonderful – provided you get between the right man and the right woman.
Woody Allen

9:18   What a blonde – she was enough to make a bishop kick a hole in a stained glass window.
Raymond Chandler

9:19   I blame my mother for my poor sex life. All she told me was 'the man goes on top and the woman underneath'. For three years my husband and I slept in bunk beds.
Joan Rivers

9:20   The Love Bird is one hundred per cent faithful to his mate – as long as they are locked together in the same cage.
Will Cuppy

9:21   There is nothing in the world like the devotion of a married woman. It's a thing no married man knows anything about.
Oscar Wilde

9:22   I'd marry again if I found a man who had fifteen million dollars, would sign over half of it to me before the marriage, and guarantee he'd be dead within a year.
Bette Davis

9:23   Women are like elephants – everyone likes to look at them
       but no one likes to have to keep one.

                                                        W.C. Fields

9:24   My best birth control now is to leave the lights on.

                                                        Joan Rivers

9:25   Happiness is watching TV at your girlfriend's house during
       a power failure.

                                                        Bob Hope

9:26   Oh Lord, give me chastity, but do not give it yet.

                                                        St Augustine

9:27   She was so ugly she could make a mule back away from an
       oat bin.

                                                        Will Rogers

9:28   Divorce is the sacrament of adultery.

                                                        Jean Guichard

9:29   What would men be without women? Scarce, sir, mighty
       scarce.

                                                        Mark Twain

9:30   Niagara Falls is the bride's second great disappointment.
                                                        Oscar Wilde

9:31   My love life is terrible. The last time I was inside a woman
       was when I visited the Statue of Liberty.

                                                        Woody Allen

9:32   How I wish that Adam had died with all his ribs in his body.
                                                        Dion Boucicault

9:33   I was actually the first birth from an inflatable woman.
                                                        Tony De Meur

9:34   I would rather go to bed with Lillian Russell stark naked
       than with Ulysses S. Grant in full military regalia.
                                                        Mark Twain

9:35   I think people should be free to engage in any sexual prac-
       tices they choose – they should draw the line at goats
       though.

                                                        Elton John

9:36   A woman's mind is cleaner than a man's – that's because she changes it more often.

Oliver Herford

9:37   A man ought not to marry without having studied anatomy, and dissected at least one woman.

Honoré De Balzac

9:38   A man who marries his mistress creates a vacancy in the position.

James Goldsmith

9:39   Sex is an act which on sober reflection one recalls with repugnance and in a more elevated mood even with disgust.

A. Schopenhauer

9:40   The trees along the banks of the Royal Canal are more sinned against than sinning.

Patrick Kavanagh

9:41   My wife is the sort of woman who gives necrophilia a bad name.

Patrick Murray

9:42   It is bad manners to begin courting a widow before she gets home from the funeral.

Seumas MacManus

9:43   Drying a widow's tears is one of the most dangerous occupations known to man.

Dorothy Dix

9:44   Boy was my wife romantic! When I first met her she used to go round with a mattress strapped to her back.

Roy Brown

9:45   Marriage is like putting your hand into a bag of snakes in the hope of pulling out an eel.

Leonardo Da Vinci

9:46   Sexual intercourse is a grossly overrated pastime; the position is undignified, the pleasure momentary and the consequences utterly damnable.

Lord Chesterfield

9:47   Every woman is entitled to a middle husband she can forget.

Adela Rogers St. Johns

9:48   I had bad luck with both my wives. The first one left me and the second one didn't.

Patrick Murray

9:49   I go from stool to stool in singles bars hoping to get lucky, but there's never any gum under any of them.

Emo Philips

9:50   Men and women, women and men. It will never work.

Erica Jong

9:51   When a man steals your wife, there is no better revenge than to let him keep her.

Sacha Guitry

9:52   So little time, so many beautiful women to make love to.

Arturo Toscanini

9:53   I am the only man in the world with a marriage licence made out 'to whom it may concern'.

Mickey Rooney

9:54   Women's intuition is the result of millions of years of not thinking.

Rupert Hughes

9:55   My wife and I pondered for a while whether to take a vacation or get a divorce. We decided that a trip to Bermuda is over in two weeks, but a divorce is something you always have.

Woody Allen

9:56   Splendid couple – slept with both of them.

Maurice Bowra

9:57   Men are superior to women. For one thing, men can urinate from a speeding car.

Will Durst

9:58   I'm dating a woman now who, evidently, is unaware of the fact.

Garry Shandling

9:59   She was stark naked except for a PVC raincoat, dress, net stockings, undergarments, shoes, rain hat and gloves.

Keith Waterhouse

71

9:60 What is wrong with a little incest? It's both handy and cheap.

James Agate

9:61 I'm a wonderful housekeeper. Every time I get a divorce, I keep the house.

Zsa Zsa Gabor

9:62 She had once heard a semi-drunken peer say on TV that marriage without infidelity was like a salad without dressing.

Keith Waterhouse

9:63 Love is temporary insanity curable by marriage.

Ambrose Bierce

9:64 Love is the delusion that one woman differs from another.

H.L. Mencken

9:65 Bisexuality doubles your chances of a date on a Saturday night.

Woody Allen

9:66 Never make a task of pleasure, as the man said when he dug his wife's grave only three feet deep.

Seumas MacManus

9:67 It doesn't matter what you do in the bedroom as long as you don't do it in the streets and frighten the horses.

Mrs Patrick Campbell

9:68 She dresses to the left.

Patrick Murray

9:69 Love is the answer – but while you're waiting for the answer, sex raises some pretty good questions.

Woody Allen

9:70 My boyfriend and I broke up. He wanted to get married and I didn't want him to.

Rita Rudner

9:71 Ten men waiting for me at the door? Send one of them home, I'm tired.

Mae West

9:72 My wife is a sex object – every time I ask for sex, she objects.
Les Dawson

9:73 When a woman behaves like a man, why doesn't she behave like a nice man?
Edith Evans

9:74 A successful man is one who makes more money than his wife can spend. A successful woman is one who can find such a man.
Lana Turner

9:75 The people I'm furious with are the women's liberationists. They keep getting up on soapboxes and proclaiming women are brighter than men. That's true, but it should be kept quiet or it ruins the whole racket.
Anita Loos

9:76 There are only about twenty murders a year in London and not all are serious – some are just husbands killing their wives.
G.H. Hatherill

9:77 Sending your girl's love letters to your rival after he has married her is one form of revenge.
Ambrose Bierce

9:78 I sold the memoirs of my sex life to a publisher – they are going to make a board game out of it.
Woody Allen

9:79 He kissed me as though he was trying to clear the drains.
Alida Baxter

9:80 My wife Mary and I have been married for forty-seven years and not once have we had an argument serious enough to consider divorce; murder, yes, but divorce, never.
Jack Benny

9:81 Some women's idea of being faithful is not having more than one man in bed at the same time.
Frederic Raphael

9:82 The main difference between men and women is that men are lunatics and women are idiots.
Rebecca West

73

9:83   Basically my wife was immature. I'd be at home in my bath and she'd come in and sink my boats.

Woody Allen

9:84   I've been married six months. She looks like a million dollars, but she only knows a hundred and twenty words and she's only got two ideas in her head. The other one is hats.

Eric Linklater

9:85   Love is just a dirty trick played on us to achieve the continuation of the species.

Somerset Maugham

9:86   A terrible thing happened to me last night again – nothing.

Phyllis Diller

9:87   I married beneath me. All women do.

Nancy Astor

9:88   I chased a woman for almost two years only to discover her tastes were exactly like mine – we were both crazy about girls.

Groucho Marx

9:89   Here's to woman! Would that we could fall into her arms without falling into her hands.

Ambrose Bierce

9:90   She said he proposed something on their wedding night that even her own brother wouldn't have suggested.

James Thurber

9:91   I like George and Harriet Grote. I like him; he's so lady-like. And I like her; she's such a perfect gentleman.

Sydney Smith

9:92   The chain of wedlock is so heavy that it takes two to carry it, sometimes three.

Alexandre Dumas

9:93   The ideal marriage consists of a deaf husband and a blind wife.

Padraig Colum

9:94   Every man should have the opportunity of sleeping with Elizabeth Taylor – and at the rate she's going, every man will.

Nicky Hilton

9:95 A nymphomaniac is a woman as obsessed with sex as the average man.

Mignon McLaughlin

9:96 My wife is as cold as the hairs on a polar bear's bum.

Les Dawson

9:97 It was so cold I almost got married.

Shelley Winters

9:98 We had gay burglars the other night. They broke in and rearranged the furniture.

Robin Williams

9:99 Despite my thirty years of research into the feminine soul, I have not yet been able to answer the great question that has never been answered: What does a woman want?

Sigmund Freud

9:100 It is impossible to obtain a conviction for sodomy from an English jury. Half of them don't believe that it can physically be done, and the other half are doing it.

Winston Churchill

9:101 Women should have labels on their foreheads saying 'Government Health Warning: women can seriously damage your brains, genitals, current account, confidence, razor blades, and good standing among your friends'.

Jeffrey Bernard

9:102 You can lead a horticulture but you can't make her think.

Dorothy Parker

9:103 Sex is just poor man's polo.

Clifford Odets

9:104 I don't see so much of Alfred any more since he got so interested in sex.

Mrs Alfred Kinsey

9:105 Marriage is a ghastly public confession of a strictly private intention.

Ian Hay

9:106 If a pretty back view won't let you catch it up, it has probably got a horrible face.

Sydney Tremayne

9:107 If there is reincarnation, I'd like to come back as Warren Beatty's fingertips.

Woody Allen

9:108 Mankind and woman unkind.

Dick Diabolus

9:109 Lady Capricorn, he understood, was still keeping open bed.

Aldous Huxley

9:110 You know, of course, that the Tasmanians, who never committed adultery, are now extinct.

Somerset Maugham

9:111 All this divorce – when I meet a man now the first thing I think about is 'Is this the sort of man I want my children to spend their weekends with?'

Rita Rudner

9:112 There is one thing I would break up over, and that is if she caught me with another woman. I wouldn't stand for that.

Steve Martin

9:113 I kissed my first woman and smoked my first cigarette on the same day: I have never had time for tobacco since.

Arturo Toscanini

9:114 If God had intended us to be nudists we would have been born with no clothes on.

Leonard Lyons

9:115 Sex is the invention of a very clever venereal disease.

David Cronenberg

9:116 When a woman, in the company of two men, addresses herself almost exclusively to one, you may be sure that she is busy beneath the table pressing the foot of the other.

Gian-Carlo Menotti

9:117 I am always looking for meaningful one-night stands.

Dudley Moore

9:118 I never understood what he saw in her until I saw her eating corn on the cob at the Caprice.

Coral Browne

9:119 It is not good for man to be alone. But oh my God, what a relief.

John Barrymore

9:120 There are a number of mechanical devices which increase sexual arousal, particularly in women. Chief among these is the Mercedes-Benz 380SL convertible.

P.J. O'Rourke

9:121 I wrote out a little list of questions for Pierre to put to the Pope about our marriage problems.

Margaret Trudeau

9:122 I'll come to your room at five o'clock. If I'm late, start without me.

Tallulah Bankhead

9:123 I can't for the life of me understand why people keep insisting that marriage is doomed. All five of mine worked out.

Peter De Vries

9:124 A woman is only a woman, but a good cigar is a smoke.

Rudyard Kipling

9:125 A woman without a man is like a fish without a bicycle.

Gloria Steinem

9:126 The happiest time of anyone's life is just after the first divorce.

John Kenneth Galbraith

9:127 Adultery? Why fool about with hamburger when you can have steak at home?

Paul Newman

9:128 I'm at the stage of life when if a girl says 'no' to me I'm profoundly grateful to her.

Woody Allen

9:129 There is nothing wrong with making love with the light on. Just make sure the car door is closed.

George Burns

9:130 She broke up with me when she found out I was sleeping with her.

Brian McCormick

9:131 Burt Reynolds once asked me to go out with him. I was in his room at the time.

Phyllis Diller

9:132 Love is a matter of chemistry – sex is simply physics.

G.M. Mark

9:133 She smoked 120 gaspers per day, swore like a fisherman, drank like a fish, and was promiscuous with men, women and Etonians.

Quentin Crisp

9:134 If you are bored with your present enemies and want to make some new ones, tell two of your women friends that they look alike.

Mignon McLaughlin

9:135 I once read an advertisement in a woman's magazine that went something like this:
Do you want him to remember you and think of you when you're not there? Always wear the same perfume when you go out with him. The sense of smell is one of the greatest memory prodders. He'll learn to associate that scent with you and think of you every time he smells it, even on someone else.
My God, does the woman think I'm a Labrador retriever?

Gilbert Harding

9:136 I have been to a funeral. I cannot describe to you the howl which the widow set up at proper intervals.

Charles Lamb

9:137 By all means marry; if you get a good wife, you'll become happy; if you get a bad one, you'll become a philosopher.

Socrates

9:138 Even if man could understand women he still wouldn't believe it.

A.W. Brown

9:139 Women now have the right to plant rolled-up dollar bills in the jockstraps of steroid-sodden male strippers.

Howard Ogden

9:140 I have never married – I find that if I come to like a young woman well enough to marry her, I also find that I have come to like her far too well to wish to see her tied to an irritable bad-tempered old boor for life.

Gilbert Harding

9:141 Sex is God's joke on human beings.

Bette Davis

9:142 Making love to Marilyn Monroe was like kissing Hitler.

Tony Curtis

9:143 My ultimate fantasy is to entice a man to my bedroom, put a gun to his head, and say 'make babies or die'.

Ruby Wax

9:144 Condemned female murderers get sheaves of offers of marriage.

George Bernard Shaw

9:145 My notion of a wife at forty is that a man should be able to change her, like a bank note, for two twenties.

Douglas Jerrold

9:146 Women are an alien race of pagans set down among us. Every seduction is a conversion.

John Updike

9:147 I have climbed the ladder of success, wrong by wrong.

Mae West

9:148 Basically I wanted a woman who was an economist in the kitchen and a whore in bed. I wound up with a woman who was a whore in the kitchen and an economist in bed.

Geoffrey Gorer

9:149 Men come of age at sixty, women at fifteen.

James Stephens

9:150 I've been in love with the same woman for forty years – if my wife ever finds out, she'll kill me.

Henny Youngman

9:151 A misogynist is a man who hates women as much as women hate each other.

H.L. Mencken

9:152 Men of every age flocked around Diana Cooper like gulls round a council tip.

John Carey

9:153 A woman's most erogenous zone is her mind.

Raquel Welch

9:154 I bequeath my entire estate to my wife on condition that she marries again. I want to be sure that there will be at least one man who will regret my death.

Heinrich Heine

9:155 Sorry Mr Frost, I sleep only with the first eleven.

Antonia Fraser

9:156 I blame my father for telling me about the birds and the bees. I was going steady with a woodpecker for two years.

Bob Hope

9:157 Why should I get married and make one woman happy when I can stay single and make hundreds happy?

Frederick Lonsdale

9:158 You may be wondering what a map of the trade winds of the North Atlantic is doing on page 134 of a book entitled *Is Sex Necessary?* We realise that in most books on sex page 134 contains a cut away cross-section of the female anatomy. In our opinion a map of the trade winds of the North Atlantic is equally useful in understanding women.

James Thurber

9:159 It was a perfect marriage – she didn't want to and he couldn't.

Spike Milligan

9:160 I would read *Playboy Magazine* more often, but my glasses keep steaming over.

George Burns

9:161 Always get married early in the morning. That way, if it doesn't work out, you haven't wasted a whole day.

Mickey Rooney

9:162 I'm not taking my wife with me to Paris because you don't take a sausage roll to a banquet.

Winston Churchill

9:163 Life is a sexually transmitted disease and the mortality rate is one hundred per cent.

R.D. Laing

9:164 I said to my husband, 'you must develop some mechanical skills, like getting out of bed'.

Phyllis Diller

9:165 Homosexuality is Nature's attempt to get rid of the soft boys by sterilising them.

F. Scott Fitzgerald

9:166 I know nothing about sex because I was always married.

Zsa Zsa Gabor

9:167 A woman's place is in the wrong.

James Thurber

9:168 A woman is like a tea bag. You can't tell how strong she is until you put her in hot water.

Nancy Reagan

9:169 My wife and I had a fight the other night. Nothing much – just two police cars.

Henny Youngman

9:170 My parents had only one argument in forty-five years. It lasted forty-three years.

Cathy Ladman

9:171 The most difficult year of marriage is the one you're in.

Franklin Pierce Jones

9:172 Doris Day is as wholesome as a bowl of cornflakes and at least as sexy.

Dwight MacDonald

9:173 I am a double bagger. Not alone does my husband put a bag over my face when we are making love but he also puts a bag over his own head in case my bag should fall off and he should have to look at me.

Joan Rivers

9:174 The height of ingratitude is the failure of Reno to erect a monument to Henry the Eighth.

Gerald F. Lieberman

9:175 That woman speaks eighteen languages and she can't say 'No' in any of them.

Dorothy Parker

9:176 An Arab and his camel are inseparable. It has been said that an Arab would give up his wife rather than give up his camel. Personally I haven't got a camel, but I think it's a great idea.

Groucho Marx

9:177 No man living knows more about women than I do – and I know nothing.

Seymour Hicks

9:178 Mr Ball? How very singular.

Thomas Beecham

9:179 I feel like a million tonight – but one at a time.

Mae West

9:180 Her grief lasted longer than I have known any widow's – three days.

Joseph Addison

9:181 I was with this girl the other night and from the way she was responding to my skillful caresses, you would have sworn she was conscious from the top of her head to the tag on her toes.

Emo Philips

9:182 It has been discovered experimentally that you can draw laughter from an audience anywhere in the world, of any class or race, simply by walking on to a stage, and uttering the words 'I am a married man'.

Ted Kavanagh

9:183 Philosophy is to the real world as masturbation is to sex.

Karl Marx

9:184 Of course prostitutes have babies – where do you think traffic wardens come from?

Dave Dutton

9:185 I have everything I had twenty years ago – except that now it's all lower.

Gypsy Rose Lee

9:186 I found a long grey hair on Kevin's jacket last night. If it's another woman's I'll kill him. If it's mine I'll kill myself.
Neil Simon

9:187 The reproduction of mankind is a great marvel and mystery. Had God consulted me in the matter, I should have advised Him to continue the generation of the species by fashioning them of clay.
Martin Luther

9:188 I'm not really a homosexual – I just help them out when they're busy.
Frank Carson

9:189 Girls are always running through my mind. They don't dare walk.
Andy Gibb

9:190 It was a man's world – then Eve arrived.
Richard Armour

9:191 Her eyes were bright brown – like a couple of cockroaches desperately swimming in two saucers of boiled rhubarb.
Gerald Kersh

9:192 I know a lot of people didn't expect our relationship to last – but we've just celebrated our two months anniversary.
Britt Eckland

9:193 My wife and I had words – but I never got to use mine.
Fibber McGee

9:194 She was a really bad-looking girl. Facially, she resembled Louis Armstrong's voice.
Woody Allen

9:195 If you want to know how old a woman is, ask her sister-in-law.
Edgar W. Howe

9:196 Sex at the age of eighty-four is a wonderful experience – especially the one in winter.
Milton Berle

9:197 A man is only as old as the women he feels.
Groucho Marx

9:198   Where would man be today if it weren't for women? In the Garden of Eden eating watermelon and taking it easy.

C. Kennedy

9:199   It's too bad that in most marriage ceremonies they don't use the word 'obey' any more. It used to lend a little humour to the occasion.

Lloyd Cory

9:200   Marry her! Impossible! You mean a part of her; he could not marry her all himself. There is enough of her to furnish wives for a whole parish. You might people a colony with her; or give an assembly with her; or perhaps take your morning's walk round her, always provided there were frequent resting-places, and you were in rude health.

Sydney Smith

9:201   Women have a much better time than men in this world. There are far more things forbidden to them.

Oscar Wilde

9:202   Recently, I've ventured into the mammal family – so that's good for my sex life.

Emo Philips

9:203   I wouldn't trust my husband with a young woman for five minutes, and he's been dead for twenty-five years.

Kathleen Behan

9:204   People in a temper often say a lot of silly things that they really mean.

Penelope Gilliat

9:205   I shrug my shoulders in despair at women who moan at the lack of opportunities and then take two weeks off as a result of falling out with their boyfriends.

Sophie Mirman

9:206   It should be a very happy marriage – they are both so in love with him.

Irene Thomas

9:207   The nearest I've been to a sexual experience lately is finding lipstick on a cafe cup.

Guy Bellamy

9:208 I have so little sex appeal my gynaecologist calls me 'sir'.
Joan Rivers

9:209 It had always seemed to Louis that a fundamental desire to take postal courses was being sublimated by other people into sexual activity.
Malcolm Bradbury

9:210 If I had been a woman I would be constantly pregnant because I simply cannot say no.
Robert Maxwell

9:211 My classmates would copulate with anything that moved, but I never saw any reason to limit myself.
Emo Philips

9:212 I do not believe in using women in combat, because females are too fierce.
Margaret Mead

9:213 Marriage is a great institution, but I'm not ready for an institution yet.
Mae West

9:214 If feminists were really serious about the movement, they would do something about their poor sisters who are forced to live on large alimony handouts from men they simply can't stand.
Lloyd Cory

9:215 When I have one foot in the grave, I will tell the whole truth about women. I shall tell it, jump into my coffin, pull the lid over me, and say 'Do what you like now'.
Leon Tolstoy

9:216 My love life is so bad I'm taking part in the world celibacy championships. I meet the Pope in the semi-finals.
Guy Bellamy

9:217 I once had a large gay following, but I ducked into an alleyway and lost him.
Emo Philips

9:218 The only time my wife and I had a simultaneous orgasm was when the judge signed the divorce papers.
Woody Allen

9:219 It was a mixed marriage. I'm human, he was a Klingon.

Carol Leifer

9:220 I've married a few people I shouldn't have, but haven't we all?

Mamie Van Doren

9:221 I'm busier than a whore working two beds.

Edgar W. Howe

9:222 If he ever makes love to me and I get to hear about it, his life won't be worth living.

Mae West

9:223 The only place men want depth in a woman is in her décolletage.

Zsa Zsa Gabor

9:224 Brains are never a handicap to a girl if she hides them under a see-through blouse.

Bobby Vinton

9:225 I have slept only with men I've been married to. How many women can make that claim?

Elizabeth Taylor

9:226 Some of the happiest marriages are when homosexuals marry upper-class ladies. The sex works, because the upper-class woman doesn't expect much, and the man just shuts his eyes and thinks of Benjamin Britten.

Jilly Cooper

9:227 Love is ideal. Marriage is real. The confusion of the two shall never go unpunished.

J.W. Von Goethe

9:228 The poor wish to be rich, the rich wish to be happy, the single wish to be married, and the married wish to be dead.

Ann Landers

9:229 Of those that were born as men, all that were cowardly and spent their life in wrongdoing were transformed at the second birth into women. Such is the origin of women and of all that is female.

Plato

9:230 Every man is thoroughly happy twice in his life: just after he has met his first love, and just after he has left his last one.
H.L. Mencken

9:231 If you are married, it takes just one to make a quarrel.
Ogden Nash

9:232 I wanted to be a sex maniac but I failed the practical.
Robert Mitchum

9:233 As a young man I used to have four supple members and one stiff one. Now I have four stiff and one supple.
Henri Duc D'Aumale

9:234 A woman gives a man just two happy days: the day he marries her, and the day he buries her.
Hipponax

9:235 As a child of eight, Mr Trout had once kissed a girl of six under the mistletoe at a Christmas party, but there his sex life had come to an abrupt halt.
P.G. Wodehouse

9:236 The difference between divorce and legal separation is that a legal separation gives a husband time to hide his money.
Johnny Carson

9:237 I was at a gay nineties party the other night. All the men were gay and all the women were ninety.
Eric Morecambe

9:238 We sleep in separate rooms, we have dinner apart, we take separate vacations. We're doing everything we can to keep our marriage together.
Rodney Dangerfield

9:239 Women love men for their defects; if men have enough of them women will forgive them everything, even their gigantic intellects.
Oscar Wilde

9:240 When a couple decide to divorce, they should inform both sets of parents before having a party and telling all their friends. This is not only courteous but practical. Parents may be very willing to pitch in with comments, criticism and malicious gossip of their own to help the divorce along.
P.J. O'Rourke

87

9:241 I wasn't kissing your daughter, sir – I was just whispering in her mouth.

Chico Marx

9:242 Why does a woman work for ten years to change a man's habits and then complain that he's not the man she married?

Barbra Streisand

9:243 I like only two kinds of men – domestic and foreign.

Mae West

9:244 After we made love he took a piece of chalk and made an outline of my body.

Joan Rivers

9:245 One of my friends who is happily married has a husband so ugly she met him when a friend sent him over to her house to cure her hiccoughs.

Phyllis Diller

9:246 After my wife died, I put my mistress into cold storage for a bit.

H.G. Wells

9:247 When a man is a bit of a woman, one does like that bit to be a lady.

G.M. Young

9:248 We've just marked our tenth wedding anniversary on the calendar and threw darts at it.

Phyllis Diller

9:249 A husband should not insult his wife in public. He should insult her in the privacy of the home.

James Thurber

9:250 It takes a lot of experience for a girl to kiss like a beginner.

Joan Rivers

9:251 An open marriage is Nature's way of telling you that you need a divorce.

Ann Landers

9:252 What do I think of volkswagens? I've been in bigger women.

Harry Kurnitz

9:253 There is no bigger fan of the opposite sex than me, and I have the bills to prove it.

Alan J. Lerner

9:254 Dammit, sir, it is your duty to get married. You can't be always living for pleasure.

Oscar Wilde

9:255 Women who can, do. Those who can't become feminists.

Bobby Riggs

9:256 There is just one remark to which there is no answer – what are you doing with my wife?

Miguel De Cervantes

9:257 What part of 'no' don't you understand?

Rita Rudner

9:258 Not a soul dropped in to see me in my little cubicle in the office for days on end. I finally solved the problem by scratching my name off the door and replacing it with the legend Gents Room.

Dorothy Parker

9:259 To be able to turn a man out into the garden and tell him to stay there until the next meal, is every woman's dream.

Virginia Graham

9:260 When we got married my wife didn't have a rag on her back – but she's got plenty of them now.

Peter Eldin

9:261 Running after women never hurt anybody – it's catching them that does the damage.

Jack Davies

9:262 The great trick with a woman is to get rid of her while she thinks she's getting rid of you.

Soren Kierkegaard

9:263 All my wife has ever taken from the Mediterranean – from that whole vast intuitive culture – are four bottles of Chianti to make into lamps, and two china condiment donkeys named Sally and Peppy.

Peter Shaffer

9:264 Now that women are jockeys, baseball umpires, atomic scientists, and business executives, maybe someday they can master parallel parking.

Bill Vaughan

9:265 My wife's idea of double parking is to park her car on top of another car.

Shelley Berman

9:266 The longest sentence you can form with two words is 'I do'.
H.L. Mencken

9:267 She did have an illegitimate baby once but it was only a little one.

Frederick Marryat

9:268 Alas, she married another. They frequently do. I hope she is happy, because I am.

Artemus Ward

9:269 Be wary, how you marry one that hath cast her rider, I mean a widow.

James Howell

9:270 Almost any man can support the girl he marries, but the problem is – what's *he* going to live on?

Joseph Salak

9:271 When we want to read the deeds that are done for love, whither do we turn? To the murder columns.
George Bernard Shaw

9:272 Women are to be excluded from the eleventh annual conker championships at Oundle. Our event would be ridiculed if women competed.

Frank Elson

9:273 She could very well pass for forty-three, in the dusk with a light behind her.

W.S. Gilbert

9:274 Annette had never been in love, although she was not without experience. She had been deflowered at seventeen by a friend of her brother on the suggestion of the latter. Nicholas would have arranged it when she was sixteen, only he needed her just then for a black mass.

Iris Murdoch

9:275 I have no time for sex. It gets in the way of the action.

Alistair MacLean

9:276 Never trust a husband too far, nor a bachelor too near.

Helen Rowland

9:277 I've never yet turned over a fig leaf that didn't have a price tag on the other side.

Saul Bellow

9:278 If you never want to see a man again say 'I love you, I want to marry you, I want to have children'. They leave skid marks.

Rita Rudner

9:279 Every good painter who aspires to the creation of genuine masterpieces should first of all marry my wife.

Salvador Dali

9:280 A woman waits motionless until she is wooed. That is how the spider waits for the fly.

George Bernard Shaw

9:281 Love is the delightful interval between meeting a girl and discovering she looks like a haddock.

John Barrymore

9:282 I never knew what real happiness was until I got married. And by then it was too late.

Max Kauffmann

9:283 Wives are people who think it's against the law not to answer the phone when it rings.

Ring Lardner

9:284 My fiancé and I are having a little disagreement. What I want is a big church wedding with bridesmaids and flowers and a no-expense-spared reception; and what he wants is to break off our engagement.

Sally Poplin

9:285 'Tis better to have loved and lost.

Alfred Tennyson

9:286 The biggest myth is that as you grow older, you gradually lose your interest in sex. This myth probably got started because younger people seem to want to have sex with each other at every available opportunity including traffic lights, whereas older people are more likely to reserve their sexual activities for special occasions such as the installation of a new Pope.

Dave Barry

9:287 This is good news; of memory, hearing, all the faculties – the last to leave us is sexual desire and the ability to make love. That means that long after we're wearing bifocals or hearing aids, we'll be making love. But we won't know with whom or why.

Jack Paar

9:288 A promiscuous person is someone who is getting more sex than you are.

Victor Lownes

9:289 Men who don't understand women fall into two groups – bachelors and husbands.

Jacques Languirand

9:290 A Casanova provides a useful special service – the best women like Rolls Royces should be delivered to the customer fully run-in.

Jilly Cooper

9:291 My wife – God bless her – was in labour for thirty-two hours, and I was faithful to her the entire time.

Jonathan Katz

9:292 Divorce is painful. There's an easy way to save yourself a lot of trouble. Just find a woman you hate and buy her a house.

Pat Paulsen

9:293 Outside every thin woman is a fat man trying to get in.

Katharine Whitehorn

9:294 If it's wet dry it. If it's dry wet it. Congratulations, you are now a gynaecologist.

Patrick Murray

9:295 She wore a low but futile décolletage.

Dorothy Parker

Media and Films

10:1   There is more joy in the newspaper world over one sinner who cuts his sweetheart's throat than over the ninety-nine just men who marry and live happily ever after.

A.P. Herbert

10:2   Television is called a medium because it is neither rare nor well done.

Ernie Kovacs

10:3   Television is very educational – every time it comes on I go into another room and read a book.

Groucho Marx

10:4   I knew Doris Day before she was a virgin.

Groucho Marx

10:5   I have a television set in every room of the house but one. There has to be some place you can go when Bob Monkhouse is on.

Benny Hill

10:6   An editor is one who separates the wheat from the chaff and prints the chaff.

Adlai Stevenson

10:7   A starlet is any girl under thirty in Hollywood who is not regularly employed in a brothel.

Ben Hecht

10:8   Dead? With the newspaper strike on, I wouldn't even consider it.

Bette Davis

10:9   Everything you read in the newspapers is absolutely true, except for that rare story of which you happen to have first-hand knowledge, which is absolutely false.

Erwin Knoll

10:10   In a mere half-century, films have gone from silent to unspeakable.

Doug Larson

10:11 There is no bad publicity, except an obituary notice.
Brendan Behan

10:12 Television is a device that permits people who haven't anything to do to watch people who can't do anything.
Fred Allen

10:13 Hollywood is an asylum run by the inmates.
Laurence Stallings

10:14 He had been kicked in the head by a mule when young, and believed everything he read in the papers.
George Ade

10:15 'Hello', he lied.
Robert Maxwell

10:16 They shot too many pictures and not enough actors.
Walter Winchell

10:17 To give an accurate and exhaustive account of that period would need a far less brilliant pen than mine.
Max Beerbohm

10:18 The reason why so many people showed up at Louis B. Mayer's funeral was because they wanted to make sure he was dead.
Samuel Goldwyn

10:19 Accuracy to a newspaper is what virtue is to a lady, except that a newspaper can always print a retraction.
Adlai Stevenson

10:20 A publisher would prefer to see a burglar in his office to a poet.
Don Marquis

10:21 I was photographed on one occasion, sitting up in an over-elaborate bed looking like a heavily doped Chinese illusion-ist.
Noel Coward

10:22 One watches David Frost with the same mixture of fascination and disgust that one looks at one's turds floating in a toilet.
Patrick Murray

10:23 Sir, I have tested your gramophone machine. It adds a new terror to life and makes death a long-felt want.

Herbert Beerbohm Tree

10:24 Television is totally in the hands of semi-articulate barbarians who can barely read an autocue.

William Rushton

10:25 After being turned down by numerous publishers, he decided to write for posterity.

George Ade

10:26 If you cannot get a job as a pianist in a brothel, you become a royal reporter.

Max Hastings

10:27 We have all passed a lot of water since then.

Samuel Goldwyn

10:28 The essence of humour is surprise; that is why you laugh when you see a joke in *Punch*.

A.P. Herbert

10:29 Now Barabbas was a publisher.

Kenneth Tynan

10:30 Barbara Cartland's eyes were twin miracles of mascara and looked like two small crows that had crashed into a chalk cliff.

Clive James

10:31 What do you mean 'we' paleface?

Tonto

10:32 Television is for appearing on, not looking at.

Noel Coward

10:33 Films should have a beginning, a middle and an end – but not necessarily in that order.

Jean-Luc Godard

10:34 Glenda Jackson has a face to launch a thousand dredgers.
Jack De Manio

10:35 I don't write for pornographic magazines or swim in sewers.
Jerry Falwell

10:36 I am about to, or I am going to die. Either expression is used.

Noah Webster

10:37 Before television, people didn't even know what a headache looked like.

D. Fields

10:38 Never argue with a man who buys ink by the gallon.

Bill Greener

10:39 The current Hollywood outbreak of rabies is due to Hedda Hopper going round biting dogs.

Edith Sitwell

10:40 I have recently been broadcasting in the interests of a breakfast food whose name for the moment escapes me.

Alexander Woollcott

10:41 The only time I use women in films is when they're either naked or dead.

Joel Silver

10:42 Never let that son of a bitch in the studio again – until we need him.

Samuel Goldwyn

10:43 I love British cinema like a doctor loves his dying patient.

Ben Kingsley

10:44 Television is still in its infancy – that's why you have to get up and change it so often.

Michael Hynes

10:45 Hollywood is a trip through a sewer in a glass-bottomed boat.

Wilson Mizner

10:46 An epic is a movie with Charlton Heston in it.

James Agate

10:47 Otto Preminger couldn't direct his little nephew to the bathroom.

Dyan Cannon

10:48 No passion in the world, no love or hate, is equal to the passion to alter someone else's copy.

H.G. Wells

10:49 My films won't send people out into the streets with axes or anything. The Shirley Temple movies are more likely to do that. After listening to *The Good Ship Lollipop*, you just gotta go out and beat up somebody. Stands to reason.

Lee Marvin

10:50 What we want is a story that starts with an earthquake and works its way up to a climax.

Samuel Goldwyn

10:51 I don't want any yes-men around me. I want everyone to tell me the truth even if it costs them their jobs.

Samuel Goldwyn

10:52 We're overpaying him but he's worth it.

Samuel Goldwyn

10:53 You can fool all of the people all of the time if the advertising is right and the budget is big enough.

Joseph E. Levine

10:54 Some are born great, some achieve greatness, and some hire public relations officers.

Daniel J. Boorstin

10:55 Imagine the Lone Ranger's surprise when many years later he discovered that 'kemo sabay' means 'horse's ass'.

Garry Larsen

10:56 Beaverbrook is so pleased to be in Government that he is like the town tart who has finally married the Mayor.

Beverley Baxter

10:57 Having the critics praise you is like having the hangman say you've got a pretty neck.

Eli Wallach

10:58 Freedom of the press is limited to those who own a newspaper.

A.J. Liebling

10:59 Being published by the Oxford University Press is rather like being married to a duchess; the honour is greater than the pleasure.

G.M. Young

10:60 Most of the time Marlon Brando sounds as if he has a mouth full of wet toilet paper.

Rex Reed

10:61 Television is a twenty-one-inch prison. I'm delighted with it because it used to be that films were the lowest form of art. Now we have something to look down on.

Billy Wilder

10:62 David Frost is the bubonic plagiarist.

Jonathan Miller

10:63 No good will come of television. The word is half Greek and half Latin.

C.P. Scott

10:64 About once a month, after dinner, I gird up my loins such as they are, take as deep a breath as I can, throw my shoulders back as far as they will go, walk into the room with the television set, boldly turn it on, picking a channel at random, and then see how long I can stand it.

James Thurber

10:65 I have a face like an elephant's behind.

Charles Laughton

10:66 I saw the sequel to the movie *Clones* and you know what? It was the same movie!

Jim Samuels

10:67 Mr Mencken has just entered a Trappist monastery in Kentucky and left strict instructions that no mail was to be forwarded. The enclosed is returned, therefore, for your archives.

H.L. Mencken

10:68 Small earthquake in Chile – not many dead.

Claud Cockburn

10:69 My movies were the kind they show in prisons and aeroplanes, because nobody can leave.

Burt Reynolds

10:70 She would be a nymphomaniac if only they could calm her down a little.

Judy Garland

10:71 The longest word in the English language is the one which follows the phrase, 'And now, a word from our sponsor'.

Hal Eaton

10:72 Every time I sell 100,000 copies of *For Whom The Bell Tolls* I will forgive a son of a bitch, and when we sell a million I will forgive Max Eastman.

Ernest Hemingway

10:73 In Hollywood, writers are considered only the first drafts of human beings.

Frank Deford

10:74 You can take all the sincerity in Hollywood, place it in the navel of a fruitfly and still have room for three caraway seeds and a producer's heart.

Fred Allen

10:75 Paint eyeballs on my eyelids and I'll sleepwalk through any picture.

Robert Mitchum

10:76 I won't eat anything that has intelligent life, but I'll gladly eat a network executive or a politician.

Marty Feldman

10:77 Jack Warner has oilcloth pockets so he can steal soup.

Wilson Mizner

10:78 Awards are like haemorrhoids; sooner or later every asshole gets some.

Frederic Raphael

10:79 Lord Beaverbrook looked like a doctor struck off the roll for performing an illegal operation.

G.M. Young

10:80 The only work I ever turned down was a cable programme called *Diving for Excrement*.

Emo Philips

10:81 I've done my bit for motion pictures – I've stopped making them.

Liberace

10:82 It's greater than a masterpiece – why it's mediocre.

Samuel Goldwyn

10:83 I'll believe in colour television when I see it in black and white.

Samuel Goldwyn

10:84 Jack Benny lived on a diet of fingernails and coffee.

May Livingstone

10:85 Hollywood is Californication.

James Montgomery

10:86 The Royal Variety performance has taken on a geriatric air. People you assumed were dead totter on the stage to wild applause.

Richard Ingrams

10:87 Reading someone else's newspaper is like sleeping with someone else's wife. Nothing seems to be precisely in the right place, and when you find what you are looking for, it is not clear then how to respond to it.

Malcolm Bradbury

10:88 If I made *Cinderella*, the audience would be looking out for a body in the coach.

Alfred Hitchcock

10:89 Hollywood is Disneyland staged by Dante. You imagine purgatory is like this except that the parking is not so good.

Robin Williams

10:90 A reporter is a man who has renounced everything in life except the world, the flesh, and the devil.

David Murray

10:91 I improve on misquotation.

Cary Grant

10:92 Jogging is for people who aren't intelligent enough to watch Breakfast Television.

Victoria Wood

10:93 I once received a letter from a mother ambitious for her daughter. It read: 'I have a perfectly beautiful daughter. She is seventeen years old, five feet three inches tall, and weighs eight stone. Do you think she might succeed in films?' I replied 'Madam, it would be impossible to say, as you did not state her width'.

Alfred Hitchcock

10:94 Hitler's original title for *Mein Kampf* was *Four and a half Years of Struggle against Lies, Stupidity and Cowardice*. Everyone needs an editor.

Tim Foote

10:95 The *Sun* and the *Mirror* have become the standard-bearers of illiteracy.

Emyr Humphreys

10:96 Only presidents, editors and people with tapeworm have the right to use the editorial 'we'.

Mark Twain

10:97 Gentlemen, I agree with you that Napoleon is a tyrant, a monster, the sworn foe of our nation. But, gentlemen – he once shot a publisher.

Thomas Campbell

10:98 Take an idiot man from a lunatic asylum and marry him to an idiot woman, and the fourth generation of the connection should be a good publisher from an American point of view.

Mark Twain

10:99 Authors should write one novel and then be put in the gas chamber.

John P. Marquand

10:100 In Los Angeles they don't throw their garbage away. They make it into television shows.

Woody Allen

10:101 Tell me, how did you love my picture?

Samuel Goldwyn

10:102 For three days after death, hair and fingernails continue to grow but phone calls taper off.

Johnny Carson

10:103 If you're a sporting star, you're a sporting star. If you don't quite make it, you become a coach. If you can't coach, you become a journalist. If you can't spell, you introduce Grandstand on a Saturday afternoon.

Desmond Lynam

Medicine and Doctors

11:1   I have the body of an eighteen year old. I keep it in the fridge.

Spike Milligan

11:2   I was under the care of a couple of medical students who couldn't diagnose a decapitation.

Jeffrey Bernard

11:3   The art of medicine consists in amusing the patient while Nature affects the cure.

Voltaire

11:4   Kilbarrack, over by Howth, my father always maintained, was the healthiest graveyard in the country, with the sea air.

Brendan Behan

11:5   Either this man is dead or my watch is stopped.

Groucho Marx

11:6   A sure cure for seasickness is to sit under a tree.

Spike Milligan

11:7   A shin is a device for finding furniture in the dark.

Colin Bowles

11:8   I'm not feeling very well – I need a doctor immediately. Ring the nearest golf course.

Groucho Marx

11:9   The operation was a complete success, but the patient died of something else.

John Chiene

11:10   Armpits lead lives of quiet perspiration.

Patrick Murray

11:11   Is there anything worn under the kilt? No, it's all in perfect working order.

Spike Milligan

11:12 My doctor gave me six months to live, but when I couldn't pay the bill he gave me six months more.

Walter Matthau

11:13 He wrote a doctor's hand – the hand which from the beginning of time has been so disastrous to the pharmacist and so profitable to the undertaker.

Mark Twain

11:14 Doctors think a lot of patients are cured who have simply quit in disgust.

Don Herold

11:15 One of the most difficult things to contend with in a hospital is the assumption on the part of the staff that because you have lost your gall bladder you have also lost your mind.

Jean Kerr

11:16 I make it a rule never to smoke more than one cigar at a time.

Mark Twain

11:17 Ordinarily he was insane, but he had lucid moments when he was merely stupid.

Heinrich Heine

11:18 My army medical consisted of two questions (i) Have you got piles? (ii) Any insanity in the family? I answered yes to both and was accepted A1.

Spike Milligan

11:19 His low opinion of medical students sprang largely from the days when he had been reading Theology at Cambridge and, on his attempt to break up a noisy party of medicals late one night, he had been forcibly administered an enema of Guinness stout.

Richard Gordon

11:20 Insanity doesn't just run in our family – it practically gallops.

Cary Grant

11:21 Condoms aren't completely safe. A friend of mine was wearing one and got hit by a bus.

Bob Rubin

11:22 My brain – that's my second favourite organ.

Woody Allen

11:23 One finger in the throat and one in the rectum make a good diagnostician.

William Osler

11:24 Anyone who goes to a psychiatrist should have his head examined.

Samuel Goldwyn

11:25 All those people with wooden legs – it's pathetic, they're not fooling anyone.

Michael Redmond

11:26 I refuse to endure months of expensive humiliation from a psychoanalyst only to be told that at the age of four I was in love with my rocking-horse.

Noel Coward

11:27 My piles bleed for you.

Herbert Beerbohm Tree

11:28 Every man catches himself in the zipper of his fly once, and only once in his lifetime.

Walt Giachini

11:29 Roses are red, violets are blue
I'm schizophrenic, and so am I.

Frank Crow

11:30 Henry the Fourth's feet and armpits enjoyed an international reputation.

Aldous Huxley

11:31 A woman went to a plastic surgeon and asked him to make her like Bo Derek. He gave her a lobotomy.

Joan Rivers

11:32 It is a poor doctor who cannot prescribe an expensive cure for a rich patient.

Sydney Tremayne

11:33 I woke up the other morning and found that everything in my room had been replaced by an exact replica. So I rang my best friend and told him that everything in my room had been replaced by an exact replica. He said 'Do I know you?'

Steven Wright

11:34 My father had a profound influence on me – he was a lunatic.

Spike Milligan

11:35 She got her looks from her father – he's a plastic surgeon.

Groucho Marx

11:36 I have just learnt about his illness; let us hope it is nothing trivial.

Irving Cobb

11:37 Medicine is my lawful wife, literature is my mistress. When I get tired of one, I spend the night with the other. It is disorderly but it isn't dull and neither of them loses anything from my infidelity.

Anton Chekhov

11:38 My psychiatrist and I have decided that when we both think I am ready, I'm going to get in my car and drive off a bridge.

Neil Simon

11:39 Before undergoing a surgical operation, arrange your temporal affairs – you may live.

Ambrose Bierce

11:40 Everyone should have a few bad habits so he'll have something he can give up if his health fails.

Franklin P. Jones

11:41 I gave up visiting my psychoanalyst because he was meddling too much in my private life.

Tennessee Williams

11:42 The best medical speciality is dermatology. Your patients never call you out in the middle of the night, they never die of the disease, and they never get any better.

Martin H. Fischer

11:43 He has been a doctor a year now and has had two patients, no, three, I think – yes it was three; I attended their funerals.

Mark Twain

11:44 When I take up assassination, I shall start with the surgeons in this city and work up to the gutter.

Dylan Thomas

11:45 A paranoid is a man who knows a little of what is going on.

William Burroughs

11:46 I have finally come to the conclusion, that a good reliable set of bowels is worth more to a man than any quantity of brains.

Josh Billings

11:47 Happiness is nothing more than health and a poor memory.

Albert Schweitzer

11:48 Tell her she can't be allowed to die in peace – it's against the rules of the hospital.

John Fisher Murray

11:49 My father invented a cure for which there was no known disease – unfortunately my mother caught the cure and died of it.

Victor Borge

11:50 Dying is a very dull dreary affair, and my advice to you is to have nothing to do with it.

Somerset Maugham

11:51 My advice if you insist on slimming – eat as much as you like, just don't swallow it.

Harry Secombe

11:52 Our doctor would never really operate unless it was absolutely necessary. He was just that way. If he didn't need the money, he wouldn't lay a hand on you.

Herb Shriner

11:53 A psychiatrist is a man who asks you a lot of expensive questions your wife asks you for nothing.

Sam Bardell

11:54 Death is just nature's way of telling you to slow down.

Dick Sharples

11:55 Neurotic means he is not as sensible as I am, and psychotic means he's even worse than my brother-in-law.

Karl Menninger

11:56 A peptic ulcer is a hole in a man's stomach through which he crawls to escape from his wife.

J.A.D. Anderson

11:57 The first sign of his approaching end was when one of my old aunts, while undressing him, removed a toe with one of his socks.

Graham Greene

11:58 First you forget names, then you forget faces. Next you forget to pull your zipper up and finally you forget to pull it down.

George Burns

11:59 The medical student is likely to be the one son of the family too weak to labour on the farm, too indolent to do any exercise, too stupid for the bar and too immoral for the pulpit.

Daniel Gilman

11:60 The trouble with Freud is that he never played the Glasgow Empire Saturday night.

Ken Dodd

11:61 Modesty has ruined more kidneys than bad liquor.

S. Morris

11:62 We are all born mad. Some remain so.

Samuel Beckett

11:63 I have myself spent nine years in a lunatic asylum and have never suffered from the obsession of wanting to kill myself; but I know that each conversation with a psychiatrist in the morning made me want to hang myself because I knew I could not strangle him.

Antonin Artaud

11:64 Show me a sane man and I will cure him for you.

Carl Jung

11:65 Have you ever had the measles, and if so, how many?

Artemus Ward

11:66 What is a human being but an ingenious assembly of portable plumbing?

Christopher Morley

11:67 A psychiatrist is a man who goes to a strip-show to watch the audience.

Mervyn Stockwood

11:68 If a doctor treats your cold, it will go away in fourteen days. If you leave it alone, it will go away in two weeks.

Gloria Silverstein

11:69 I don't mind dying; the trouble is you feel so bloody stiff the next day.

George Axlerod

11:70 Are you all right? You should have two of everything down the sides and one of everything down the middle.

Ken Dodd

11:71 Doctors prescribe medicines of which they know little, to cure diseases of which they know less, in human beings of which they know nothing.

Voltaire

11:72 Running through the park I had a bad asthmatic attack – three asthmatics jumped me. It was my own fault – I should have heard them hiding.

Emo Philips

11:73 Psychoanalysis is the disease it purports to cure.

Karl Kraus

11:74 I was a caesarean birth but you can't really tell, except that every time I leave the house I go out by the window.

Steven Wright

11:75 I didn't know the full facts of life until I was seventeen. My father never talked about his work.

Martin Freud

11:76 Nature is that lovely lady to whom we owe polio, leprosy, smallpox, syphilis, tuberculosis and cancer.

Stanley N. Cohen

11:77 A male gynaecologist is like an auto mechanic who has never owned a car.

Carrie Snow

11:78 William Wilde, father of Oscar Wilde and a noted eye specialist, operated on the father of George Bernard Shaw to correct a squint, and overdid the correction so much that the unfortunate man squinted the other way for the rest of his life.

Hesketh Pearson

11:79 Among the side effects of this drug, the most significant is the immediate death of the patient.

Philip Mason

11:80 Exercise is bunk. If you are healthy, you don't need it; if you are sick, you shouldn't take it.

Henry Ford

11:81 The trouble with heart disease is that the first symptom is often hard to deal with – sudden death.

Michael Phelps

11:82 I'm not crazy, but I think everyone else is.

Peter O'Toole

11:83 The only parts left of my original body are my elbows.

Phyllis Diller

11:84 Just because you are paranoid doesn't mean they aren't out to get you.

Patrick Murray

11:85 Jumping into the sea is a certain cure for seasickness.

John Ruskin

11:86 The great art of a quack is to time his imposture.

Richard Duppa

11:87 He is alive, but only in the sense that he cannot be legally buried.

Geoffrey Madan

11:88 The nicest present I ever got was an exploding suppository.

Emo Philips

11:89 One out of four people is mentally unbalanced. Think of your three closest friends. If they seem OK then you're the one.

Ann Landers

11:90 There must be something to acupuncture – after all, you never see any sick porcupines.

Bob Goddard

11:91 There are more men than women in mental hospitals which just goes to show who's driving who crazy.

Peter Veale

11:92 I slept well only once in my life, and even then I dreamt I was awake.

Irving Berlin

11:93 Happiness is a warm bed pan.

Christopher Hudson

11:94 A good patient is one who, having found a good doctor, sticks to him until he dies.

Oliver Wendell Holmes

11:95 Knocked down a doctor? With an ambulance? How could she? It's a contradiction in terms.

N.F. Simpson

11:96 There's another advantage of being poor – a doctor will cure you faster.

Kin Hubbard

11:97 One would think that in an age of unemployed doctors, the British Medical Association might support the noble art of boxing on the grounds that it provides more work for them. Instead they have voted to ban the sport altogether.

Auberon Waugh

11:98 Cyclists represent only one per cent of the traffic, but they account for ten per cent of the traffic deaths. We physicians call cyclists 'organ donors'.

Cheryl Winchell

11:99 I've lost six pounds on the way to the Super Bowl. Mind you, that's like throwing a deck chair off the Queen Mary.

Bill Parcells

11:100 When I meet a man whose name I cannot remember, I give myself two minutes, then if it is a hopeless case I always say 'And how is the old complaint?'

Benjamin Disraeli

11:101 While quacks normally kill you, doctors merely allow you to die.

Jean De La Bruyere

11:102 My dear doctor, I'm surprised to hear you say that I am coughing very badly, because I have been practising all night.

John Philpot Curran

11:103 Poor old Lord Mortlake, who had only two topics of conversation, his gout and his wife. I never could quite make out which of the two he was talking about.

Oscar Wilde

11:104 Except for an occasional heart attack I feel as young as I ever did.

Robert Benchley

11:105 The only weapon with which the unconscious patient can immediately retaliate upon the incompetent surgeon is the haemorrhage.

W.S. Halstead

11:106 Talk of the patience of Job, said a hospital nurse, Job was never on night duty.

Stephen Paget

11:107 The secret of longevity is to keep breathing.

Sophie Tucker

11:108 He collected lists of fatal diseases and arranged them in alphabetical order so that he could put his finger without delay on any one he wanted to worry about.

Joseph Heller

11:109 I've already had medical attention – a dog licked me while I was on the ground.

Neil Simon

11:110 A successful doctor needs three things. A top hat to give him authority; a paunch to give him dignity, and piles to give him an anxious expression.

Samuel Johnson

11:111 A grave is a place where the dead are laid to await the coming of the medical student.

Ambrose Bierce

11:112 If your time hasn't come, not even a doctor can kill you.

M.A. Perlstein

11:113 There are three natural anaesthetics – sleep, fainting and death.

Oliver Wendell Holmes

11:114 Mr Anaesthetist, if the patient can stay awake, surely you can.

Wilfred Trotter

11:115 I have a perfect cure for a sore throat – cut it.

Alfred Hitchcock

Music

12:1 The music teacher came twice a week to bridge the awful gap between Dorothy and Chopin.

George Ade

12:2 The bagpipes are an instrument of torture consisting of a leaky bag and punctured pipes, played by blowing up the bag and placing the fingers over the wrong holes.

Dick Diabolus

12:3 Most rock journalism is people who cannot write interviewing people who cannot talk for people who cannot read.

Frank Zappa

12:4 Jazz is music invented for the torture of imbeciles.

Henry Van Dyke

12:5 I could eat alphabet soup and shit better lyrics than that.

Johnny Mercer

12:6 A violin is the revenge exacted by the intestines of a dead cat.

Ambrose Bierce

12:7 The Mafia once moved in and took over the New York Ballet. During a performance of 'Swan Lake', there was a lot of money on the swan to live.

Woody Allen

12:8 Brass bands are all very well in their place – outdoors and several miles away.

Thomas Beecham

12:9 Swans sing before they die – 'twere no bad thing did certain persons die before they sing.

S.T. Coleridge

12:10 Classical music is the kind you keep thinking will turn into a tune.

Kin Hubbard

12:11　I have never heard any Stockhausen, but I do believe I have stepped in some.

Thomas Beecham

12:12　Wagner has some lovely moments but some terrible quarters of an hour.

Gioacchino Rossini

12:13　The harpsichord sounds like two skeletons copulating on a corrugated tin roof.

Thomas Beecham

12:14　She was a town-and-country soprano of the kind often used for augmenting grief at a funeral.

George Ade

12:15　The Sydney Opera House looks as if it were something that had crawled out of the sea and was up to no good.

Beverley Nichols

12:16　One cannot judge Wagner's opera *Lohengrin* after a first hearing and I have no intention of sitting through it a second time.

Gioacchino Rossini

12:17　Wagner's music is better than it sounds.

Mark Twain

12:18　Having adapted Beethoven's Ninth Symphony for *Fantasia*, Walt Disney commented 'Gee, this'll make Beethoven'.

Marshall McLuhan

12:19　The third movement of Bartok's Fourth Quartet began with a dog howling at midnight, proceeded to imitate the regurgitations of the less refined type of water-closet and concluded with the cello reproducing the screech of an ungreased wheelbarrow.

Alan Dent

12:20　I find that distance lends enchantment to bagpipes.

William Blezard

12:21　Please do not shoot the pianist – he's doing his best.

Oscar Wilde

12:22　I liked your opera. I think I will set it to music.

Ludwig Van Beethoven

114

12:23 I write music as a sow piddles.

W.A. Mozart

12:24 I'm a concert pianist. That's a pretentious way of saying I'm unemployed at the moment.

Oscar Levant

12:25 A highbrow is anyone who can listen to the William Tell Overture and not think of The Lone Ranger.

Jack Perlis

12:26 We will now have the Second Dance Rhapsody of Frederick Delius, a work which was given some years ago and of which we shall now hear the first performance.

Thomas Beecham

12:27 Wagner is the Puccini of music.

J.B. Morton

12:28 Why do we in England engage at our concerts so many third-rate continental conductors when we have so many second-rate ones of our own?

Thomas Beecham

12:29 It is sobering to consider that when Mozart was my age he had already been dead for a year.

Tom Lehrer

12:30 Bagpipes are the missing link between music and noise.

E.K. Kruger

12:31 Others, when the bagpipe sings i' the nose, cannot contain their urine.

William Shakespeare

12:32 If that's what the top twenty records sound like, I shudder to think what the bottom fifty must sound like.

C. Street

12:33 The third movement of Beethoven's Seventh Symphony is like a lot of yaks jumping about.

Thomas Beecham

12:34 Sleep is an excellent way of listening to an opera.

James Stephens

12:35 Crooning is a reprehensible form of singing that established itself in light entertainment mainly about the 1930s. It recommended itself at first to would-be singers without voices who were unable to acquire an adequate technique. The principle of crooning is to use as little voice as possible and instead to make a sentimental appeal by prolonged moaning somewhere near the written notes.

Eric Blom

12:36 Opera is when a guy gets stabbed in the back and instead of bleeding he sings.

Edward Gardner

12:37 Critics can't even make music by rubbing their back legs together.

Mel Brooks

12:38 *Parsifal* is the kind of opera that starts at 6 o'clock. After it has been going on for three hours you look at your watch and it says 6.20.

David Randolph

12:39 Mr Robin Day asks me to vouch for the fact that he can sing. I testify that the noise he makes is in fact something between that of a rat drowning, a lavatory flushing and a hyena devouring her after-birth in the Appalachian Mountains under a full moon.

Auberon Waugh

12:40 My favourite two composers are the Bachs-Johann Sebastian and Jacques Offen.

Victor Borge

12:41 The best tune of *Evita*, the already famous 'Don't Cry for me Argentina', is inferior as a melody to the ones I used when a boy to hear improvised on a saxophone outside the Albert Hall by a busker with only three fingers on his left hand.

Bernard Levin

12:42 There are seventy verses in the Uruguay national Anthem, which fact may account for the Uruguay standing army.

Franklin P. Adams

12:43 Anybody who has listened to certain kinds of music, or read certain kinds of poetry, or heard certain kinds of performances on the concertina, will admit that even suicide has its brighter aspects.

Stephen Leacock

12:44 If bullshit was music, that fellow would be a brass band.
Paddy Crosbie

12:45 After the United States premiere of *Salome*, the critics went up into the attic and dusted off adjectives that hadn't been in use since Ibsen was first produced in London. I remember that 'bestial,' 'fetid', 'slimy', and 'nauseous' were among the more complimentary terms.
Deems Taylor

12:46 The inventor of the bagpipes was inspired when he saw a man carrying an indignant asthmatic pig under his arm. Unfortunately, the manmade sound never equalled the purity of the sound achieved by the pig.
Alfred Hitchcock

12:47 His Majesty does not know what the Grenadier Guards Band has just played, but it is never to be played again.
King George V

12:48 No operatic tenor has yet died soon enough for me.
Thomas Beecham

12:49 I wish the Government would put a tax on pianos for the incompetent.
Edith Sitwell

12:50 I don't like composers who think. It gets in the way of their plagiarism.
Howard Dietz

12:51 You made me love you, I didn't want to do it. You woke me up to do it.
Sammy Kahn

12:52 I have a very simple secret about playing the piano. I sit down on the piano stool and I make myself comfortable – and I always make sure that the lid over the keyboard is open before I start to play.
Artur Schnabel

12:53 'Spinning Wheel' by Blood, Sweat and Tears, is music to commit voluntary euthanasia by.
Simon Hoggart

12:54 If there is anyone here whom I have not insulted, I beg his pardon.

Johannes Brahms

12:55 You know what you do when you shit? Singing it's the same thing, only up!

Enrico Caruso

12:56 His vibrato sounded like he was driving a tractor over ploughed fields with weights tied to his scrotum.

Spike Milligan

12:57 The true gentleman is a man who knows how to play the bagpipes but doesn't.

Thomas Beecham

12:58 Bring not a bagpipe to a man in trouble.

Jonathan Swift

12:59 I knew a Russian peasant who could make his horse micturate by whistling softly. That same whistling sound I have heard in several pieces of electronic music, and it makes me suffer the same desire as the horse.

Igor Stravinsky

12:60 When Phyllis Diller started to play, Steinway came down personally and rubbed his name off the piano.

Bob Hope

12:61 You must play Chopin to me. The man with whom my wife ran away played Chopin exquisitely.

Oscar Wilde

12:62 Last year I gave several lectures on 'Intelligence and the appreciation of Music among Animals'. Today I am going to speak to you about 'Intelligence and the appreciation of Music among Critics.' The subjects are very similar.

Eric Satie

12:63 If there is music in hell it will be bagpipes.

Joe Tomelty

12:64 Modern music is the noise made by deluded speculators picking through the slagpile.

Henry Pleasants

12:65 Schoenberg would be better off shovelling snow.

Richard Strauss

Nationalities and Places

13:1   In England there are a hundred religions and only one sauce which is melted butter.

Francesco Caracciolo

13:2   Note the tower, which is said to be the sixth highest in East Anglia.

Stephen Potter

13:3   Canada could have enjoyed English government, French culture and American know-how. Instead it ended up with English know-how, French government and American culture.

John Robert Colombo

13:4   The Irish gave the bagpipes to the Scots as a joke, but the Scots haven't seen the joke yet.

Oliver Herford

13:5   I am willing to love all mankind, except an American.

Samuel Johnson

13:6   People don't actually swim in Dublin Bay – they are merely going through the motions.

Brendan Behan

13:7   I would like to live in Manchester, England. The transition between Manchester and death would be unnoticeable.

Mark Twain

13:8   Always remember that you are an Englishman and therefore have drawn first prize in the lottery of life.

Cecil Rhodes

13:9   The first item on the agenda of every Irish organisation is 'The Split'.

Brendan Behan

13:10 It is no longer true that Continentals have a sex life whereas the English have hot-water bottles – the English now have electric blankets.

George Mikes

13:11 In Pierre Trudeau Canada has at last produced a political leader worthy of assassination.

Irving Layton

13:12 America is the only nation in history which miraculously has gone from barbarism to degeneracy without the usual interval of civilisation.

Georges Clemenceau

13:13 The bars in Dublin are shut from 2.30 to 3.30. We call it the Holy Hour. The politician who introduced it was shot an hour afterwards.

Brendan Behan

13:14 Once you've been on a plane full of drunken Australians doing wallaby imitations up and down the aisles, you'll never make fun of Americans again.

P.J. O'Rourke

13:15 The main difference between Los Angeles and yogurt is that yogurt has an active living culture.

Tom Taussik

13:16 There are still parts of Wales where the only concession to gaiety is a striped shroud.

Gwyn Thomas

13:17 Of course America had often been discovered before Columbus, but it had always been hushed up.

Oscar Wilde

13:18 For breakfast, the first morning I was in France, I had a steaming bidet of coffee, followed by porridge and frogs.

Spike Milligan

13:19 The English have sex on the brain – which is a frightfully uncomfortable place to have it.

Malcolm Muggeridge

13:20 In Paris they simply stared when I spoke to them in French; I never did succeed in making those idiots understand their own language.

Mark Twain

13:21 I have a great admiration for Mussolini, who has welded a nation out of a collection of touts, blackmailers, ice-cream vendors and gangsters.

Michael Bateman

13:22 The war situation has developed not necessarily to Japan's advantage.

Emperor Hirohito (1945)

13:23 Much may be made of a Scotchman, if he be caught young.

Samuel Johnson

13:24 A great many people in Los Angeles are on strict diets that restrict their intake of food. The reason for this appears to be a widely-held belief that organically grown fruit and vegetables make the cocaine work faster.

Fran Lebowitz

13:25 We must keep America whole and safe and unspoiled.

Al Capone

13:26 She lived in France – that country to which lesbianism is what cricket is to England.

Quentin Crisp

13:27 America is the land of permanent waves and impermanent wives.

Brendan Behan

13:28 I know only two words of American slang; 'swell' and 'lousy'. I think 'swell' is lousy, but 'lousy' is swell.

J.B. Priestley

13:29 It requires a surgical operation to get a joke into a Scotch understanding.

Sydney Smith

13:30 The high standards of Australians are due to the fact that their ancestors were all hand-picked by the best English judges.

Douglas Copland

13:31 I don't hold with abroad and think that foreigners speak English when our backs are turned.

Quentin Crisp

13:32 Those comfortably padded lunatic asylums which are known, euphemistically, as the stately homes of England.

Virginia Woolf

13:33 The noblest prospect which a Scotchman ever sees is the high road that leads him to England.

Samuel Johnson

13:34 There are over thirty words in the Irish language which are equivalent to the Spanish 'manana'. But somehow none of them conveys the same sense of urgency.

Patrick Kavanagh

13:35 When St Patrick drove the snakes out of Ireland, they swam to New York and joined the police force.

Eugene O'Neill

13:36 I have been trying all my life to like Scotchmen, and am obligated to desist from the experiment in despair.

Charles Lamb

13:37 Canada is useful only to provide me with furs.

Madame De Pompadour

13:38 Americans are a race of convicts and ought to be thankful for anything we allow them short of hanging.

Samuel Johnson

13:39 No man is thoroughly miserable unless he is condemned to live in Ireland.

Jonathan Swift

13:40 The English winter – ending in July, to recommence in August.

George Gordon

13:41 In Ireland a girl has the choice between perpetual virginity and perpetual pregnancy.

George Moore

13:42 The French invented the only known cure for dandruff. It is called the guillotine.

P.G. Wodehouse

13:43 Your proper child of Caledonia is the bandy-legged lout from Tullietudlesleugh, who, after a childhood of intimacy with the cesspool and the crablouse, and twelve months at 'the college' on moneys wrung from the diet of his family, drops his threadbare kilt and comes south in a slop suit to instruct the English in the arts of civilisation and in the English language.

T.W. Crosland

13:44 He was so depressed, he tried to commit suicide by inhaling next to an Armenian.

Woody Allen

13:45 Australia is a country whose industrial and commercial development has been unspeakably retarded by an unfortunate dispute among geographers as to whether it is a continent or an island.

Ambrose Bierce

13:46 The ignorance of French society gives one a rough sense of the infinite.

Joseph Ernest Renan

13:47 The sun never sets on the British Empire because God wouldn't trust an Englishman in the dark.

Duncan Spaeth

13:48 The softer the currency in a foreign country, the harder the toilet paper.

John Fountain

13:49 The Irish climate is wonderful, but the weather ruins it.

Tony Butler

13:50 To be a Frenchman abroad is to be miserable; to be an American abroad is to make other people miserable.

Ambrose Bierce

13:51 We had a very successful trip to Russia – we got back.

Bob Hope

13:52 A gesticulation is any movement made by a foreigner.

J.B. Morton

13:53 What do I think of Western civilisation? I think it would be a very good idea.

Mahatma Ghandi

13:54 When the missionaries came to Africa they had the Bible and we had the land. They said 'Let us pray'. We closed our eyes. When we opened them we had the Bible and they had the land.

Desmond Tutu

13:55 Nebraska is proof that hell is full and the dead walk the earth.

Liz Winston

13:56 Black Englishmen and women who win Olympic medals are described as English while those who riot and throw petrol bombs are invariably West Indian.

Edward Hughes

13:57 The English find ill-health not only interesting but respectable, and often experience death in the effort to avoid a fuss.

Pamela Frankau

13:58 It must be marvellous to be a man and just cheerfully assume I was superior. Better still, I could be an Irishman and have all the privileges of being male without giving up the right to be wayward, temperamental and an appealing minority.

Katharine Whitehorn

13:59 The English never smash in a face. They merely refrain from asking it to dinner.

Margaret Halsey

13:60 I have to choose between this world, the next world and Australia.

Oscar Wilde

13:61 In the Soviet Union a writer who is critical is taken to a lunatic asylum. In the United States, he is taken to a talk show.

Carlos Fuentes

13:62 When in Paris, I always eat at the Eiffel Tower restaurant because it's the only place where I can avoid seeing the damned thing.

William Morris

13:63 It is unthinkable for a Frenchman to arrive at middle age without having both syphilis and the Cross of the Legion of Honour.

Andre Gide

13:64 The US embassy in Moscow is nothing but an eight-storey microphone plugged into the Politburo.

Richard Armey

13:65 It is peculiar that all the sights in Rome are called after London cinemas.

Nancy Mitford

13:66 I never met anyone in Ireland who understood the Irish question, except one Englishman who had only been there a week.

Kenneth Fraser

13:67 One of the girls in my swimming squad complained that there were men in the women's changing room, only to discover on investigation that she had merely overheard East German girls in the next cubicle.

Charles Wilson

13:68 Going to the loo in a yacht in a French harbour is not so much goodbye as au revoir.

Noel Coward

13:69 An Iranian moderate is one who believes that the firing squad should be democratically elected.

Henry Kissinger

13:70 When an Englishman is totally incapable of doing any work whatsoever, he describes himself on his income-tax form as a 'gentleman'.

Robert Lynd

13:71 I never believed in Santa Claus because I knew no white dude would come into a black neighbourhood after dark.

Dick Gregory

13:72 In January, the Americans announce a new invention. In February, the Russians announce they made the same discovery 20 years ago. In March, the Japanese start exporting the invention to the U.S.

Lloyd Cory

13:73 My rackets are run on strictly American lines and they're going to stay that way.

Al Capone

13:74 I went to Paris and stayed at the Hotel Demolition by Kirkpatrick.

Spike Milligan

13:75 There are three things to beware of: the hoof of a horse, the horn of a bull, and the smile of an Englishman.

Seumas MacManus

13:76 When asked his opinion of Welsh nationalism, Mr Thomas replied in three words, two of which were 'Welsh nationalism.'

Dylan Thomas

13:77 When I die I want to decompose in a barrel of porter and have it served in all the pubs in Dublin.

J.P. Donleavy

13:78 The great majority of Germans, realising the practical impossibility of speaking their own language with any degree of success, abandon it altogether and communicate with one another on brass bands.

Frank Richardson

13:79 I am not British. On the contrary.

Samuel Beckett

13:80 In Istanbul I was known as 'English Delight'.

Noel Coward

13:81 No bombardment of Rheims Cathedral can do anything like the damage that the last restoration did.

Roger Fry

13:82 The Great Wall, I've been told, is the only man-made structure on earth that is visible from the moon. For the life of me I cannot see why anyone would go to the moon to look at it, when, with almost the same difficulty, it can be viewed in China.

J.K. Galbraith

13:83 You gotta say this for the white race – its self-confidence knows no bounds. Who else could go to a small island in the South Pacific where there is no poverty, no crime, no unemployment, no war and no worry – and call it a 'primitive society'.

Dick Gregory

13:84 Americans are remorseless. They invite you to a party. You can't say 'I've got a splitting headache' – they'll send the doctor around.

V.S. Pritchett

13:85 American newspapers are too big, and their lavatory paper is too small.

Ernest Bevin

13:86 It is never difficult to distinguish between a Scotsman with a grievance and a ray of sunshine.

P.G. Wodehouse

13:87 Heaven is an English policeman, a French cook, a German engineer, an Italian lover and everything organised by the Swiss. Hell is an English cook, a French engineer, a German policeman, a Swiss lover and everything organised by the Italians.

John Elliot

13:88 America has become so tense and nervous, it's been years since I've seen anyone asleep in church.

Norman Vincent Peale

13:89 My ancestors were Puritans from England. They arrived in the United States in 1648 in the hope of finding greater restrictions than were permissible under English law at that time.

Garrison Keillor

13:90 I was in a library in Toronto in 1915, studying a Latin poet, and all of a sudden I thought, war can't be this bad. So I walked out and enlisted.

Lester B. Pearson

13:91 I was the toast of two continents – Greenland and Australia.

Dorothy Parker

13:92 In Italy for thirty years under the Borgias they had warfare, terror, murder, bloodshed, but they produced Michelangelo, Leonardo da Vinci, and the Renaissance. In Switzerland, they had brotherly love, they had five hundred years of democracy and peace. And what did they produce? The cuckoo-clock.

Orson Welles

13:93 The only time in his life that Joseph Joffre, French marshal, ever put up a fight was when asked for his resignation.

Winston Churchill

13:94 To live in Australia permanently is rather like going to a party and dancing all night with your mother.

Barry Humphries

13:95 Canada is a country so square that even the female impersonators are women.

Richard Brenner

13:96 The Welsh are the only nation in the world that has produced no graphic or plastic art, no architecture, no drama. They just sing. Sing and blow down instruments of plated silver.

Evelyn Waugh

13:97 New Zealand is a country of thirty thousand million sheep – three million of whom think they are human.

Barry Humphries

13:98 Sex is allowed in Scotland only when Rangers beat Celtic.

Ronnie Barker

13:99 Cork, like Dublin, possesses a river, but there is no record that any Cork townsman has ever succeeded in spitting across it. This is not to say that the townsmen of Cork have given up trying. Indeed, some Cork townsmen endeavour to keep themselves in practice even when their beautiful river is not in sight.

Shamus O'Shamus

13:100 I once heard a Welsh sermon in which the word 'truth' was repeatedly uttered in English. Apparently there is no exact equivalent in Welsh.

Geoffrey Madan

13:101 In Ireland when the weather forecast is bad, it's invariably correct; when it's good, it's invariably wrong.

Tony Butler

13:102 My opinion of New York is that the newspapers are too thick and the lavatory paper too thin.

Winston Churchill

13:103 The purpose of an introduction in England is to conceal the identities of two people from each other.

George Mikes

13:104 One Russian is an anarchist, two Russians are a chess game, three Russians are a revolution, and four Russians are the Budapest String Quartet.

Jascha Heifetz

13:105 If it was raining soup, the Irish would be out with forks.

Brendan Behan

13:106 Wales is the land of my fathers. And my fathers can have it.

Dylan Thomas

13:107 We can trace almost all the disasters of English history to the influence of Wales.

Evelyn Waugh

13:108 The British tourist is always happy abroad as long as the natives are waiters.

Robert Morley

13:109 I like the English. They have the most rigid code of immorality in the world.

Malcolm Bradbury

13:110 Apart from cheese and tulips, the main product of Holland is advocaat, a drink made from lawyers.

Alan Coren

13:111 The United States, I believe, are under the impression that they are twenty years in advance of Britain; whilst, as a matter of actual verifiable fact, they are just about six hours behind it.

Harold Hobson

13:112 On the Continent, people have good food; in England people have good table manners.

George Mikes

13:113 I shook hands with a friendly Arab – I still have my right hand to prove it.

Spike Milligan

13:114 Life is too short to learn German.

Richard Porson

13:115 In India, a farm hand was caught in the act with his cow. He said he had bad eyesight and thought it was his wife.

Spike Milligan

13:116 They say that men become attached even to Widnes.

A.J. Taylor

13:117 It is good to be on your guard against an Englishman who speaks French perfectly; he is likely to be a card sharp or an attache in the diplomatic service.

Somerset Maugham

13:118 Homosexuality in Russia is a crime, and the punishment is seven years in prison, locked up with the other men. There is a three year waiting list.

Yakov Smirnoff

13:119 I had always imagined that cliche was a suburb of Paris, until I discovered it was a street in Oxford.

Philip Guedalla

13:120 On entering an English railway carriage it is customary to shake hands with all the passengers.

R. J. Phillips

13:121 Have you tried the famous echo in the Reading Room of the British Museum?

Gerard Hoffnung

13:122 Where but in Kenya can a man whose grandfather was a cannibal watch a really good game of polo?

Marina Sulzberger

13:123 The British may not be the greatest nation at winning Winter Olympics, but at least we can carry our bloody flag properly.

Mike Freeman

13:124 Names are not always what they seem. The common Welsh name BZJXXLLWCP is pronounced Jackson.

Mark Twain

13:125 Americans hardly ever retire from business; they are either carried out feet first or they jump from a window.

A.L. Goodheart

13:126 The devil will not come to Cornwall, for fear of being put into a pie.

Clement Freud

13:127 The Germans take part of a verb and put it down here, like a stake, and then they take the other part of it and put it over yonder like another stake, and between these two limits they just shovel in German.

Mark Twain

13:128 For some reason, a glaze passes over people's faces when you say Canada.

Sondra Gotlieb

13:129 The world still consists of two clearly divided groups; the English and the foreigners. One group consists of less than 50 million people; the other of 3,950 million. The latter group does not really count.

George Mikes

13:130 Students of Soviet affairs know how difficult it is to foretell the Soviet past.

George Paloczi-Horvath

13:131 The French have just invented a Michelin bomb – it destroys only restaurants with less than four stars.

Robin Williams

13:132 Russian comedians must be careful about what jokes they tell. If you say 'Take my wife, please,' when you get home, she's gone.

Yakov Smirnoff

13:133 As for marriage, it is one of America's most popular institutions. The American man marries early and the American woman marries often; and they get on extremely well together.

Oscar Wilde

13:134 A French Member of Parliament went to sleep for half an hour during a debate and when he woke he found he had been Prime Minister twice.

Oswald Lewis

13:135 Dutch is not so much a language as a disease of the throat.
Mark Twain

13:136 How about the raffle where the first prize was a week in Belfast and the second prize was a fortnight in Belfast.
Brendan Behan

Politics

14:1   The ideal form of government is democracy tempered with assassination.

Voltaire

14:2   Democracy is a pathetic belief in the collective wisdom of individual ignorance.

H.L. Mencken

14:3   I never trust a man unless I've got his pecker in my pocket.

Lyndon B. Johnson

14:4   Sure let him join our campaign. I'd prefer to have him inside our tent pissing out than outside our tent pissing in.

Lyndon B. Johnson

14:5   It is true that liberty is precious – so precious it must be carefully rationed.

V.I. Lenin

14:6   The cardinal rule of politics – never get caught in bed with a live man or a dead woman.

Larry Hagman

14:7   I do not belong to any organised political party – I am a Democrat.

Will Rogers

14:8   The main difference for the history of the world if I had been shot rather than Kennedy, is that Onassis probably wouldn't have married Mrs Khrushchev.

Nikita Khrushchev

14:9   It is now known that men enter local politics solely as a result of being unhappily married.

C.N. Parkinson

14:10   The Tories are nothing else but a load of kippers, two-faced with no guts.

Eric Heffer

14:11 The draft is white people sending black people to fight yellow people to protect the country they stole from red people.

James Rado

14:12 I never vote for anyone – I always vote against.

W.C. Fields

14:13 Watergate was the only brothel where the madam remained a virgin.

Mort Sahl

14:14 A fool and his money are soon elected.

Will Rogers

14:15 An honest politician is one who when he is bought, stays bought.

Simon Cameron

14:16 I don't make jokes. I just observe the government and report the facts.

Will Rogers

14:17 O.K. I will come back from Brazil to reunite Europe. But no nice boy tactics this time.

Adolf Hitler

14:18 No comment, but don't quote me.

Dan Quayle

14:19 My family was in Irish politics while De Valera's was still bartering budgerigars on the back streets of Barcelona.

James Dillon

14:20 A statesman is a dead politician. We need more statesmen.

Bob Edwards

14:21 Stanley Baldwin is dead – the light in that great turnip has at last gone out.

Winston Churchill

14:22 A debate without the honourable member would be like *Hamlet* without the third grave digger.

Winston Churchill

14:23 Reader suppose you were an idiot; and suppose you were a member of Congress; but I repeat myself.

Mark Twain

14:24 I do not see the EEC as a great love affair. It is more like nine middle-aged couples with failing marriages meeting at a Brussels hotel for a group grope.

Kenneth Tynan

14:25 The government has been faced with an orchestrated campaign of pressures by the newspapers. They even had the gargantuan intellect of Bernard Levin squeaking away in the undergrowth like a demented vole.

Denis Healey

14:26 If you don't say anything you won't be called on to repeat it.

Calvin Coolidge

14:27 One of the things that being in politics has taught me is that men are not a reasoned or a reasonable sex.

Margaret Thatcher

14:28 Sir Robert Peel's smile is like the silver fittings on a coffin. The Right Honourable Gentleman is reminiscent of a poker. The only difference is that a poker gives off occasional signs of warmth.

Benjamin Disraeli

14:29 The difference between a misfortune and a calamity is this: if Gladstone fell into the Thames, it would be a misfortune. But if someone dragged him out again, that would be a calamity.

Benjamin Disraeli

14:30 All political parties die at last of swallowing their own lies.

John Arbuthnot

14:31 I'm glad I'm not Brezhnev. Being the Russian leader in the Kremlin, you never know if someone's tape-recording what you say.

Richard M. Nixon

14:32 Richard Nixon told us he was going to take crime off the streets. He did. He took it into the White House.

Ralph Abernathy

14:33 The speeches of Warren Harding left the impression of an army of pompous phrases moving over the landscape in search of an idea. Sometimes these meandering words would actually capture a straggling thought and bear it triumphantly a prisoner in their midst, until it died of servitude and overwork.

William McAdoo

14:34 During Stalin's speeches to the Praesidium, the first delegate to stop clapping was routinely hauled off to be shot.

Clive James

14:35 The purpose of the Presidential Office is not power, or leadership of the Western World, but reminiscence, bestselling reminiscence.

Roger Jellinek

14:36 Sometimes I look at Billy and Jimmy and I say to myself 'Lillian, you should have stayed a virgin'.

Lillian Carter

14:37 Actually, I vote Labour – but my butler's Tory.

Louis Mountbatten

14:38 Chamberlain seemed such a nice old gentleman that I thought I would give him my autograph.

Adolf Hitler

14:39 He has all the characteristics of a dog except loyalty.

Sam Houston

14:40 You'll notice that Nancy Reagan never drinks water when Ronnie speaks.

Robin Williams

14:41 Some Republicans are so ignorant they wouldn't know how to pour piss out of a boot – even if the instructions were printed on the heel.

Lyndon B. Johnson

14:42 When the President does it, that means it's not illegal.

Richard M. Nixon

14:43 Tony Benn is the Bertie Wooster of Marxism.

Malcolm Bradbury

14:44 Gerald Ford looks like the guy in a science fiction movie who is first to see the Creature.

David Frye

14:45 The Vice-Presidency isn't worth a pitcher of warm spit.

J.N. Garner

14:46 A politician is any citizen with influence enough to get his old mother a job as a charwoman in the City Hall.

H.L. Mencken

14:47 It's easy being a humorist when you've got the whole government working for you.

Will Rogers

14:48 I like Republicans, and I would trust them with anything in the world except public office.

Adlai Stevenson

14:49 I am sorry that I cannot address the people of Latin America in their own language which is Latin.

Dan Quayle

14:50 Stanley Baldwin occasionally stumbled over the truth, but hastily picked himself up and hurried on as if nothing had happened.

Winston Churchill

14:51 Richard Nixon is a no-good, lying bastard. He can lie out of both sides of his mouth at the same time, and if he ever caught himself telling the truth, he'd lie just to keep his hand in.

Harry S. Truman

14:52 An aristocracy in a republic is like a chicken whose head has been cut off: it may run about in a lively way, but in fact it is dead.

Nancy Mitford

14:53 He who throws mud loses ground.

Adlai Stevenson

14:54 When you say that you agree to a thing in principle you mean that you have not the slightest intention of carrying it out in practice.

Otto Von Bismarck

14:55 Chamberlain has the mind and manner of a clothes-brush.
Harold Nicholson

14:56 Ronald Reagan has done for monetarism what the Boston Strangler did for door-to-door salesmen.
Denis Healey

14:57 A committee is a group of people who individually can do nothing, but together decide that nothing can be done.
Fred Allen

14:58 Richard Needham is a man who, having escaped from the *Titanic*, has clambered aboard the *Marie Celeste*.
Peter Sharpe

14:59 Arthur Scargill couldn't negotiate his way out of a toilet.
Ray Lynk

14:60 The Liberals are Dr Barnado's home for orphan voters.
Gerry Neale

14:61 Paul Channon is educated beyond his intelligence.
Dennis Skinner

14:62 The Social Democrats are the heterosexual wing of the Liberal Party.
George Foulkes

14:63 An ambassador is a person who, having failed to secure an office from the people, is given one by the Administration on condition that he leave the country.
Ambrose Bierce

14:64 I have no interest in sailing round the world. Not that there is any lack of requests for me to do so.
Edward Heath

14:65 A philosopher Tory, like military intelligence, is a contradiction in terms.
Michael Foot

14:66 The right honourable gentleman is indebted to his memory for his jests, and to his imagination for his facts.
Richard Brinsley Sheridan

14:67 I never drink coffee at lunch – I find it keeps me awake for the afternoon.

Ronald Reagan

14:68 The government solution to any problem is usually at least as bad as the problem.

Milton Friedman

14:69 To err is Truman.

Walter Winchell

14:70 A committee is a group of the unwilling, picked from the unfit, to do the unnecessary.

Richard Harkness

14:71 All animals are equal but some are more equal than others.

George Orwell

14:72 Apart from that Mrs Lincoln, how did you enjoy the play?

Tom Lehrer

14:73 Given half a chance, politicians would give lower taxes and extra social security concessions to marginal constituencies only.

William Keegan

14:74 William Whitelaw is one of the last representatives of a dying Tory tradition – possession of land, enthusiasm for shooting small birds, and antipathy for reading books.

Roy Hattersley

14:75 Politics is the art of choosing between the disastrous and the unpalatable.

John K. Galbraith

14:76 Neil Kinnock looks like a tortoise having an orgasm.

Patrick Murray

14:77 I wouldn't believe that Hitler was dead, even if he told me himself.

Hjalmar Schacht

14:78 Clement Attlee reminds me of nothing so much as a dead fish before it has time to stiffen.

George Orwell

14:79 The Labour Party's election manifesto is the longest suicide note in history.

Greg Knight

14:80 I don't know what I would do without Whitelaw. Everyone should have a Willy.

Margaret Thatcher

14:81 I always have one golden rule for such occasions – I ask myself what Nanny would have expected me to do.

Lord Carrington

14:82 Put three Zionists in a room – and they will form four political parties.

Levi Eshkol

14:83 Now and then an innocent man is elected to the legislature.

Frank McKinney

14:84 I met Lord Curzon in Downing Street and received from him the sort of greeting a corpse would give to an undertaker.

Stanley Baldwin

14:85 I want it so that you can't wipe your ass on a piece of paper that hasn't got my picture on it.

Lyndon B. Johnson

14:86 Neville Chamberlain might make an adequate Lord Mayor of Birmingham – in a lean year.

David Lloyd-George

14:87 The function of socialism is to raise suffering to a higher level.

Norman Mailer

14:88 Revolution is a trivial shift in the emphasis of suffering.

Tom Stoppard

14:89 Winston Churchill would kill his own mother just so that he could use her skin to make a drum to beat his own praises.

Margot Asquith

14:90 When more and more people are thrown out of work unemployment results.

Calvin Coolidge

14:91 Politics is the art of looking for trouble, finding it every-where, diagnosing it wrongly and applying unsuitable remedies.

Ernest Benn

14:92 I don't know what people have got against the government – they've done nothing.

Bob Hope

14:93 An infallible method of conciliating a tiger is to allow oneself to be devoured.

Konrad Adenauer

14:94 McKinley has about as much backbone as a chocolate eclair.

Theodore Roosevelt

14:95 The illegal we do immediately. The unconstitutional takes a little longer.

Henry Kissinger

14:96 Politicians are wedded to the truth, but like many other married couples they sometimes live apart.

H.H. Munro

14:97 De Valera discloses the workings of a mind to which incoherence lends an illusion of profundity.

T. De Vere-White

14:98 Ted Heath is a politician past his sell by date.

Neil Kinnock

14:99 Get all the fools on your side and you can be elected to anything.

Frank Dane

14:100 I haven't heard from our ambassador to Spain in three years. If he doesn't contact me in the next year, I intend to write.

George Washington

14:101 A typical speech by Margaret Thatcher sounds like the *Book of Revelations* read over a railway station public address system by a headmistress of a certain age wearing calico knickers.

Clive James

14:102 Robert Muldoon is a bull who carries his own china shop with him.

Inder Jit

14:103 The voters have spoken – the bastards.

Richard Nixon

14:104 Winston Churchill never spares himself in conversation. He gives himself so generously that hardly anybody else is permitted to give anything in his presence.

Aneurin Bevan

14:105 Intervening in Gerald Ford's re-election campaign is like re-arranging the deck chairs on the *Titanic*.

Rogers Morton

14:106 Harold Wilson is going around the country stirring up apathy.

William Whitelaw

14:107 He stood twice for Parliament, but so diffidently that his candidature passed almost unnoticed.

Evelyn Waugh

14:108 If you would know the depth and meanness of human nature, you have got to be a prime minister running a general election.

John A. MacDonald

14:109 I always wanted to get into politics, but I was never light enough to make the team.

Art Buchwald

14:110 If you walk like a duck, and you quack like a duck, and you say you're a duck, you are a duck.

George Bush

14:111 Ninety per cent of the politicians give the other ten per cent a bad reputation.

Henry Kissinger

14:112 I have reason to believe that the fowl pest outbreaks are the work of IRA.

Ian Paisley

14:113 Walter Mondale has all the charisma of a speed bump.

Will Durst

14:114 So Reagan consults an astrologer – I'm glad he consults somebody.

Jim Wright

14:115 I have always found F.D. Roosevelt an amusing fellow, but I would not employ him, except for reasons of personal friendship, as a geek in a common carnival.

Murray Kempton

14:116 I am extraordinarily patient, provided I get my own way in the end.

Margaret Thatcher

14:117 George Washington was ignorant of the commonest accomplishments of youth. He could not even lie.

Mark Twain

14:118 A year ago Gerald Ford was unknown throughout America. Now he's unknown throughout the world.

Norman Mailer

14:119 The supporters I value are those who will support me when I am wrong. Anyone can support me when I am right.

W.L. Melbourne

14:120 I have orders to be awakened at any time in case of a national emergency, even if I'm in a cabinet meeting.

Ronald Reagan

14:121 There are only three men who have ever understood the Schleswig-Holstein question. One was Prince Albert, who is dead. The second was a German professor, who became mad. I am the third and I have forgotten all about it.

Viscount Palmerston

14:122 Mr Lloyd George spoke for a hundred and seventeen minutes, in which period he was detected only once in the use of an argument.

Arnold Bennett

14:123 I have not met Norman Scott face to face for many years.

Jeremy Thorpe

14:124 He may be a son of a bitch, but at least he's our son of a bitch.

Franklin Roosevelt

14:125 Who is King Billy? Go home man and read your Bible.

Ian Paisley

14:126 One could drive a prairie schooner through any part of the arguments of William Jennings Bryan and never scrape against a fact.

David Huston

14:127 I have only two regrets – that I have not shot Henry Clay or hanged John C. Calhoun.

Andrew Jackson

14:128 Charles De Gaulle looked like a female llama surprised in her bath.

Winston Churchill

14:129 Republicans sleep in twin beds, some even in separate rooms. That's why there are more Democrats.

Walt Stanton

14:130 As for the look on Dan Quayle's face – how to describe it? If a tree fell in a forest, and no one was there to hear it, it might sound like Dan Quayle looks.

Tom Shales

14:131 Stanley Baldwin – one could not even dignify him with the name of stuffed shirt. He was simply a hole in the air.

George Orwell

14:132 The Secret Service is under orders that if Bush is shot, to shoot Quayle.

John Kerry

14:133 If the word 'No' was removed from the English language, Ian Paisley would be speechless.

John Hume

14:134 If Nixon's secretary, Rosemary Woods, had been Moses' secretary, there would only have been eight commandments.

Art Buchwald

14:135 Ninety-nine per cent of the adults in this country are decent, hard-working, honest Americans. It's the other lousy one per cent that gets all the publicity and gives us a bad name. But then, we elected them.

Lily Tomlin

14:136 Nixon impeached himself. He gave us Gerald Ford as revenge.

Bella Abzug

14:137 The more you read about politics, the more you have got to admit that each party is worse than the other.

Will Rogers

14:138 The League of Nations is like sheep passing resolutions in favour of vegetarianism.

Dean Inge

14:139 At every crisis the Kaiser crumpled. In defeat, he fled; in revolution he abdicated; in exile he remarried.

Winston Churchill

14:140 The House of Lords is a model of how to care for the elderly.

Frank Field

14:141 For socialists, going to bed with the Liberals is like having oral sex with a shark.

Larry Zolf

14:142 I am thoroughly in favour of Mrs Thatcher's visit to the Falklands. I find a bit of hesitation, though, about her coming back.

John Mortimer

14:143 Communism is the lay form of Catholicism.

George Bernard Shaw

14:144 The British Labour Party is more Methodist than Marxist.

Morgan Phillips

14:145 The US communist party was at one stage so heavily infiltrated by FBI undercover agents that they outnumbered the actual communists.

Louis Heren

14:146 Keith Joseph is a mixture of Rasputin and Tommy Cooper.

Denis Healey

14:147 There cannot be a world crisis next week, my schedule is full.

Henry Kissinger

14:148 My one ardent desire is that after the war Lloyd George should be publicly castrated in front of Edith Cavell's statue.

Lytton Stracey

14:149 The British Secret Service was staffed at one period almost entirely by alcoholic homosexuals working for the KGB.

Clive James

14:150 I know I'm getting better at golf because I'm hitting fewer spectators.

Gerald R. Ford

14:151 Everywhere in England and America statesmen were already preparing their triumphs of 1914 and 1939, by spending long days on the golf course and long nights at the bridge table.

Osbert Sitwell

14:152 Have you ever noticed how England wins the World Cup only under a Labour government?

Harold Wilson

14:153 There is a man standing at the bottom of Niagara Falls trying to push the water back with his hands. He is Public Relations Officer to the Prime Minister and the Cabinet.

William Connor

14:154 The Labour Party have lost the last four elections. If they lose another, they get to keep the Liberal Party.

Clive Anderson

14:155 Stafford Cripps has a first rate mind until he makes it up.

Violet Asquith

14:156 Richard Nixon was offered $2 million by Schick to do a television commercial for Gillette.

Gerald R. Ford

14:157 When they circumcised Herbert Samuel, they threw away the wrong bit.

David Lloyd-George

14:158 A committee is a cul-de-sac into which ideas are lured and then quietly strangled.

Barnett Cocks

14:159 Ronald Reagan is a triumph of the embalmer's art.

Gore Vidal

14:160 They think that whenever anyone in the White House now tells a lie I get a royalty.

Richard M. Nixon

14:161 Ronald Reagan won because he ran against Jimmy Carter. If he had run unopposed he would have lost.

Mort Sahl

14:162 I am still heavyweight champion of Uganda. Nobody is willing to fight me.

Idi Amin

14:163 President Calvin Coolidge was the greatest man ever came out of Plymouth Corner, Vermont.

Clarence Darrow

Religion

15:1 Not only is there no God, but try getting a plumber at weekends.

Woody Allen

15:2 God made everything out of nothing. But the nothingness shows through.

Paul Valéry

15:3 The men who really believe in themselves are all in lunatic asylums.

G.K. Chesterton

15:4 A good sermon should be like a woman's skirt: short enough to rouse the interest, but long enough to cover the essentials.

Ronald Knox

15:5 Peter remained on friendly terms with Christ even though Christ had healed his mother-in-law.

Samuel Butler

15:6 How can I believe in God when only last week I got my tongue caught in the roller of an electric typewriter?

Woody Allen

15:7 The trouble with most of us is that we have been inoculated with small doses of Christianity in childhood which keeps us from catching the real thing.

Bob Phillips

15:8 He was of the faith chiefly in the sense that the church he currently did not attend was Catholic.

Kingsley Amis

15:9 I don't believe in astrology because I'm a Gemini, and Geminis never believe in astrology.

Raymond Smullyan

15:10 Millions long for immortality who do not know what to do with themselves on a rainy Sunday afternoon.

Susan Ertz

15:11 Woman was God's second mistake.

Friedrich Nietzsche

15:12 As God once said, and I think rightly ...

Margaret Thatcher

15:13 I'm astounded by people who want to 'know' the universe when it's so hard to find your way around Chinatown.

Woody Allen

15:14 I do benefits for all religions – I'd hate to blow the hereafter on a technicality.

Bob Hope

15:15 Some people say there is a God; others say there is no God. The truth probably lies somewhere in between.

W. B. Yeats

15:16 Philosophy is unintelligible answers to insoluble problems.

Henry B. Adams

15:17 I have spent a lot of time searching through the Bible for loopholes.

W.C. Fields

15:18 The Bible tells us to love our neighbours, and also to love our enemies; probably because they are generally the same people.

G.K. Chesterton

15:19 I'm really a timid person – I was beaten up by Quakers.

Woody Allen

15:20 Sir, a woman preaching is like a dog walking on its hind legs. You don't expect it to be done well – you are surprised to find it done at all.

Samuel Johnson

15:21 An atheist is a guy who watches a Notre Dame versus SMU football game and doesn't care who wins.

Dwight D. Eisenhower

15:22 On the question of eternal punishment, the word 'eternal' did not appear to the elders of St Osoph's to designate a sufficiently long period of time.

Stephen Leacock

15:23 Hearing nuns' confessions is like being stoned to death with popcorn.

Fulton J. Sheen

15:24 I have tried in my time to be a philosopher, but cheerfulness always kept breaking in.

Oliver Edwards

15:25 The word *good* has many meanings. For example, if a man were to shoot his grandmother at a range of five hundred yards, I should call him a good shot, but not necessarily a good man.

G.K. Chesterton

15:26 Thank God I'm an atheist.

Luis Bunuel

15:27 The Bible was a consolation to a fellow alone in the old cell. The lovely thin paper with a bit of mattress stuffing in it, if you could get a match, was as good a smoke as ever I tasted.

Brendan Behan

15:28 Become a Protestant? Certainly not. Just because I've lost my faith doesn't mean I've lost my reason.

James Joyce

15:29 If you want to make God laugh, tell him your future plans.

Woody Allen

15:30 Why do born again people so often make you wish they had never been born the first time?

Katharine Whitehorn

15:31 I do not believe in an after life, although I am bringing a change of underwear.

Woody Allen

15:32 The Anglo-Saxon conscience doesn't stop you from sinning; it just stops you from enjoying it.

Salvador De Madariaga

15:33 How was I to know that the Pope was a Catholic? Nobody's infallible.

George Brown

15:34 Only one man ever understood me – and he didn't understand me.

G.W. Hegel

15:35 They say that Joseph Smith did not receive from the hands of an angel the written revelation that we obey. Let them prove it!

Brigham Young

15:36 I desire to go to hell and not to heaven. In the former place I shall enjoy the company of Popes, Kings and Princes, while in the latter are only beggars, monks and apostles.

Niccolo Machiavelli

15:37 An archbishop is an ecclesiastical dignitary one point holier than a bishop.

Ambrose Bierce

15:38 He is such a devout Catholic, he won't be happy until he is crucified.

John B. Keane

15:39 One of the crying needs of the time is for a suitable Burial Service for the admittedly damned.

H.L. Mencken

15:40 Life is the ever dwindling period between abortion and euthanasia.

Patrick Murray

15:41 I haven't been to Mass for years. I've got every mortal sin on my conscience, but I know when I'm doing wrong. I'm still a Catholic.

Angus Wilson

15:42 The sewing-circle is the Protestant confessional, where each one confesses, not her own sins, but the sins of her neighbours.

Charles B. Fairbanks

15:43 When I was a kid, I used to pray every night for a new bicycle. Then I realised that the Lord doesn't work that way, so I just stole one and asked Him to forgive me.

Emo Philips

15:44 I'm a communist by day and a Catholic after it gets dark.

Brendan Behan

15:45   Few sinners are saved after the first twenty minutes of a sermon.

Mark Twain

15:46   Monica Baldwin's book *I Leapt over the Wall* strengthened my desire not be become a nun.

Noel Coward

15:47   Malcolm Muggeridge was a thief crucified between two Christs.

Anthony Powell

15:48   Plenty well, no pray. Big bellyache, heap God.

Geronimo

15:49   The secret of a good sermon is to have a good beginning and a good ending and having the two as close together as possible.

George Burns

15:50   Things have come to a pretty pass when religion is allowed to invade the sphere of private life.

W.L. Melbourne

15:51   I would have made a good Pope.

Richard M. Nixon

15:52   Where would Christianity be if Jesus had got eight to fifteen years with time off for good behaviour?

James Donovan

15:53   I expect you know my friend Evelyn Waugh, who, like you, your Holiness is a Roman Catholic.

Randolph Churchill

15:54   There is a species of person called a 'Modern Churchman' who draws the full salary of a beneficed clergyman and need not commit himself to any religious belief.

Evelyn Waugh

15:55   I know I am God because when I pray to him I find I'm talking to myself.

Peter Barnes

15:56 I never quite forgave Mahaffy for getting himself suspended from preaching in the College Chapel. Ever since his sermons were discontinued, I suffer from insomnia in church.

George Tyrrell

15:57 Would you, my dear young friends, like to be inside with the five wise virgins, or outside, alone and in the dark with the five foolish ones?

Montagu Butler

15:58 I never heard him cursing; I don't believe he was ever drunk in his life – sure he's not like a Christian at all.

Sean O'Casey

15:59 I was brought up in a clergyman's household, so I am a first-class liar.

Sybil Thorndyke

15:60 It is a sin to believe in the evil of others, but it is seldom a mistake.

H.L. Mencken

15:61 My ancestors wandered lost in the wilderness for forty years because even in biblical times men would not stop to ask for directions.

Elayne Boosler

15:62 God is love, but get it in writing.

Gypsy Rose Lee

15:63 I was raised in the Jewish tradition, taught never to marry a Gentile woman, shave on a Saturday night and, most especially, never to shave a Gentile woman on a Saturday night.

Woody Allen

15:64 Maybe this world is another planet's hell.

Aldous Huxley

15:65 When we talk to God, we're praying. When God talks to us we're schizophrenic.

Lily Tomlin

15:66 Eternal torment is almost certain for the vast majority: but a very few may hope for merciful annihilation.

Hugh Cecil

15:67 The *Revised Prayer Book* is an attempt to suppress burglary by legalising petty larceny.

Dean Inge

15:68 Lies are defensible in the face of an attempt to extract personal information by direct question.

John Henry Newman

15:69 There is a lost Scottish community, long unable to read or write. They preserve one relic only of Protestantism, that if they get hold of any meat, they keep it until Friday to eat.

G.M. Young

15:70 The Commandments don't tell you what you ought to do: they only put ideas into your head.

Elizabeth Bibesco

15:71 Perhaps the most lasting pleasure in life is the pleasure of not going to church.

Dean Inge

15:72 Jesus was born on a bank holiday and died on a bank holiday. We can therefore assume that when he returns again it will also be on a bank holiday.

P. G. Johnson

15:73 I don't pray because I don't want to bore God.

Orson Welles

15:74 I must believe in the Apostolic Succession, there being no other way of accounting for the descent of the Bishop of Exeter from Judas Iscariot.

Sydney Smith

15:75 A church is a place in which clergymen who have never been to heaven preach about it to people who will never get there.

H.L. Mencken

15:76 There are three sexes – men, women and clergymen.

Sydney Smith

15:77 The three great elements of modern civilisation were gunpowder, printing, and the Protestant Religion.

Thomas Carlyle

154

15:78 Sleep is good, death is better; but the best thing would be never to have been born at all.

Heinrich Heine

15:79 How could God do this to me after all I've done for him?

King Louis XIV

15:80 When a woman gets too old to be attractive to man, she turns to God.

Honoré De Balzac

15:81 I once heard of a prophet who, when he baptised converts, at night, in a deep river, also drowned them, so that, being cleaned of sin and having no time to sin again, they went straight to Paradise.

Joyce Cary

15:82 I have noticed again and again since I have been in the church that lay interest in ecclesiastical matters is often a prelude to insanity.

Evelyn Waugh

15:83 Moss Hart's elegant country house and grounds are just what God would have done if He had the money.

Alexander Woollcott

15:84 Vouchsafe O Lord, to keep us this day without being found out.

Samuel Butler

15:85 Mr Kremlin himself was distinguished for his ignorance, for he had only one idea and that was wrong.

Benjamin Disraeli

15:86 All are lunatics, but he who can analyse his delusions is called a philosopher.

Ambrose Bierce

15:87 If you want to make a man very angry, tell him you are going to pray for him.

Edgar W. Howe

15:88 I'm Jewish. I don't work out. If God had wanted us to bend over, He would have put diamonds on the floor.

Joan Rivers

15:89 There is not the least use in preaching to anyone unless you chance to catch them ill.

Sydney Smith

15:90 I am increasingly convinced that the *Church Times* is now edited by the Devil in person.

Bishop Gore

15:91 The principal reason for the increase in the number of misprints in literature is the increasingly liberal attitude of the Church of England. Not enough parsons are unfrocked these days. The unfortunates of earlier days were often happy to find themselves employment in printing houses, correcting proofs.

David Holloway

15:92 'Meet my daughter', said the bishop, with some disgust.

Evelyn Waugh

15:93 'Take my camel, dear,' said my Aunt Dot, as she climbed down from this animal on her return from High Mass.

Rose MacAulay

15:94 A dead atheist is someone who's all dressed up with nowhere to go.

James Duffecy

15:95 A Calvinistic Presbyterian believes that all Catholics will be damned because they are predestined to be damned; an ordinary Presbyterian believes that all Catholics will be damned on their merits.

John Bartley

15:96 What do people say when God sneezes?

Henny Youngman

15:97 I'm not Jewish – it's just that a tree fell on me.

Spike Milligan

15:98 Give me a no-nonsense down to earth behaviourist, a few drugs and simple electrical appliances, and in six months I will have him reciting the Athaniasian creed in public.

W.H. Auden

15:99 God can stand being told by Professor Ayer and Margharita Laski that He does not exist.

J.B. Priestley

15:100 The Bible tells us to forgive our enemies; not our friends.

Margot Asquith

15:101 The most scandalous charges against the Pope were suppressed. His Holiness was accused only of piracy, rape, murder, sodomy and incest.

Edward Gibbon

Science and Technology

16:1 Ouch!

Isaac Newton

16:2 In ancient times they had no statistics so they had to fall back on lies.

Stephen Leacock

16:3 The speed at which boiling milk rises from the bottom of the pan to any point beyond the top is greater than the speed at which the human brain and hand can combine to snatch the confounded thing off.

H.F. Ellis

16:4 Statistics are like loose women; once you get your hands on them you can do anything you like with them.

Walt Michaels

16:5 An expert is someone who has made all the mistakes that can be made, but in a very narrow field.

Niels Bohr

16:6 Everybody talks about the weather, but nobody does anything about it.

Charles D. Warner

16:7 It is impossible to combine the heating of milk with any other pursuit whatever.

H.F. Ellis

16:8 How does the little busy bee improve each shining hour and gather honey all the day from every opening flower? Well, he does not. He spends most of the day in buzzing and aimless acrobatics, and gets about a fifth of the honey he would collect if he organised himself.

Heneage Ogilvie

16:9 He uses statistics as a drunken man uses a lamp post – more for support than illumination.

Andrew Lang

16:10 To pray is to ask that the laws of the universe be annulled on behalf of a single petitioner confessedly unworthy.

Ambrose Bierce

16:11 Descended from the apes? Let us hope that is not true. But if it is, let us pray that it may not become generally known.

F.A. Montagu

16:12 Living on Earth may be expensive, but it includes an annual free trip around the sun.

Ashleigh Brilliant

16:13 Ketchup left overnight on dinner plates has a longer half-life than radioactive waste.

Wes Smith

16:14 How do they get that non-stick stuff to stick to the frying pan?

Steven Wright

16:15 Why don't they make the whole plane out of that black box stuff?

Steven Wright

16:16 Computer dating is fine – if you're a computer.

Rita May Brown

16:17 You can have a Model T Ford car any colour you like, so long as it's black.

Henry Ford

16:18 Get your facts right first and then you can distort them as much as you please.

Mark Twain

16:19 Smoking is one of the leading causes of statistics.

Fletcher Knebel

16:20 There are lies, damn lies, and statistics.

Mark Twain

16:21 Outer space is no place for a person of breeding.

Violet Bonham Carter

16:22 I put some instant coffee in the microwave oven the other night and I got a time reversal.

Steven Wright

16:23 We've got to take the atom bomb seriously – it's dynamite.
Samuel Goldwyn

16:24 The guy who invented the first wheel was an idiot, but the guy who invented the other three, now he was a genius.
Sid Caesar

16:25 I bought some batteries, but they weren't included.
Steven Wright

16:26 The scientific theory I like best is that the rings of Saturn are composed entirely of lost airline luggage.
Mark Russell

16:27 If there had been a computer in 1872 it would have predicted that by now there would be so many horse-drawn vehicles that the entire surface of the earth would be ten feet deep in horse manure.
Karl Kapp

16:28 Biologically speaking, if something bites you, it is more likely to be female.
Desmond Morris

16:29 I knew immediately when I had reached the North Pole, because in one step the north wind became a south wind.
Robert Peary

16:30 He was a good citizen, an upright man, and an ardent patriot, but of limited information regarding circular saws.
Stephen Leacock

16:31 Computers are improving – perhaps even to the point of writing poetry as good as that composed by a drunken poet.
Louis T. Milic

16:32 Asking an aerospace worker if he's ever been laid off before is like asking a mother if she's ever had a baby.
Richard Kapusta

16:33 Anybody who says he's been eaten by a wolf is a liar.
J.B. Theberge

16:34 All sorts of computer errors are now turning up. You'd be surprised to know the number of doctors who claim they are treating pregnant men.
Isaac Asimov

16:35 Damn the Solar System. Bad light; planets too distant, pestered with comets; feeble contrivance; could make better myself.

Francis Jeffery

16:36 Hell must be isothermal, for otherwise the resident engineers and physical chemists (of whom there must be many) could set up a heat engine to run a refrigerator to cool off a portion of their surroundings to any desired temperature.

Henry A. Bent

16:37 To err is human, but to really foul things up you need a computer.

Paul Ehrlich

16:38 When I die, I'm going to leave my body to science fiction.

Steven Wright

16:39 I have a seashell collection; maybe you've seen it? I keep it on beaches all over the world.

Steven Wright

16:40 The most useful and least expensive household repair tool is the telephone.

Wes Smith

16:41 When you've seen one Redwood, you've seen 'em all.

Ronald Reagan

16:42 Science has conquered many diseases, broken the genetic code and even placed human beings on the moon, yet when a man of eighty is left in a room with two eighteen year-old cocktail waitresses, nothing happens. Because the real problems never change.

Woody Allen

Social Behaviour and Manners

17:1   In my experience, if you have to keep the lavatory door shut by extending your left leg, it's modern architecture.

Nancy Banks-Smith

17:2   The general advertiser's attitude would seem to be: if you are a lousy, smelly, idle, under-privileged, overweight and over-sexed status-seeking neurotic moron, give me your money.

Kenneth Bromfield

17:3   Style is when they're running you out of town and you make it look like you're leading a parade.

William Battie

17:4   An acquaintance is someone we know well enough to borrow from but not well enough to lend to.

Ambrose Bierce

17:5   There are many who dare not kill themselves for fear of what the neighbours will say.

Cyril Connolly

17:6   As far as I'm concerned there are only two kinds of people in the world – those who are kind to their servants and those who are not.

Duke of Argyll

17:7   I told the traffic warden to go forth and multiply, though not exactly in those words.

Woody Allen

17:8   As yet, Bernard Shaw hasn't become prominent enough to have any enemies; but none of his friends like him.

Oscar Wilde

17:9   There is only one immutable law in life – in a gentleman's toilet, incoming traffic has the right of way.

Hugh Leonard

17:10 It is illegal to make liquor privately or water publicly.

Lord Birkett

17:11 Know him? I know him so well that I haven't spoken to him for ten years.

Oscar Wilde

17:12 The full potentialities of human fury cannot be reached until a friend of both parties tactfully intervenes.

G.K. Chesterton

17:13 He was a great patriot, a humanitarian, a loyal friend – provided of course he really is dead.

Voltaire

17:14 Don't touch a woman's knee at the dinner table; she has an instinctive knowledge whether a man who touches her knee is caressing her or only wiping his greasy fingers on her stocking.

George Moore

17:15 Always forgive your enemies. Nothing annoys them so much.

Oscar Wilde

17:16 The only thing I really mind about going to prison is the thought of Lord Longford coming to visit me.

Richard Ingrams

17:17 Whatever you have read I have said is almost certainly untrue, except if it is funny in which case I *definitely* said it.

Tallulah Bankhead

17:18 If any reader of this book is in the grip of some habit of which he is deeply ashamed, I advise him not to give way to it in secret but to do it on television. No one will pass him with averted gaze on the other side of the street. People will cross the road at the risk of losing their own lives in order to say 'We saw you on the telly'.

Denis Pratt

17:19 I once sent a dozen of my friends a telegram saying FLEE AT ONCE – ALL IS DISCOVERED.
They all left town immediately.

Mark Twain

17:20   Anyone can do any amount of work provided it isn't the work he is supposed to be doing at the moment.

Robert Benchley

17:21   A pessimist is a man who, when he smells flowers, looks around for the coffin.

H.L. Mencken

17:22   When you have to kill a man it costs nothing to be polite.

Winston Churchill

17:23   I am free of all prejudice. I hate everyone equally.

W.C. Fields

17:24   When little men cast long shadows, the sun is about to set.

Michael Seymour

17:25   There is nothing like the sight of an old enemy down on his luck.

Euripides

17:26   If you cannot say anything good about someone, sit right here by me.

Alice Roosevelt

17:27   Those who give up smoking aren't the heroes. The real heroes are the rest of us – who have to listen to them.

Hal Boyle

17:28   I do not have to forgive my enemies – I have had them all shot.

Ramon Narvaez

17:29   Wit is like caviar. It should be served in small elegant portions and not splashed about like marmalade.

Noel Coward

17:30   One should never be unnecessarily rude to a lady except in street cars.

O. Henry

17:31   Blown his brains out you say? He must have been an incredibly good shot.

Noel Coward

17:32 I have a most peaceable disposition. My desires are for a modest hut, a thatched roof, a good bed, good food, very fresh milk and butter, flowers in front of my window and a few pretty trees by my door. And should the good Lord wish to make me really happy, he will allow me the pleasure of seeing about six or seven of my enemies hanged upon those trees.

Heinrich Heine

17:33 I regret very much my inability to attend your banquet. It is the baby's night out and I must stay at home with the nurse.

Ring Lardner

17:34 If this is the way that Queen Victoria treats her prisoners, she doesn't deserve to have any.

Oscar Wilde

17:35 It is perfectly monstrous the way people go about nowadays saying things against one, behind one's back, that are absolutely and entirely true.

Oscar Wilde

17:36 The louder he talked of his honour, the faster we counted our spoons.

R.W. Emerson

17:37 It is well known that if you stop and wind the window down to ask someone the way, he invariably turns out to be either deaf, senile, or a stranger there himself.

Lambert Jeffries

17:38 People often say to me 'What are you doing in my garden?'

Michael Redmond

17:39 Never murder a man when he's busy committing suicide.

Woodrow Wilson

17:40 If only these old walls could talk, how boring they would be.

Robert Benchley

17:41 I must decline your invitation owing to an engagement I am just about to make.

Oscar Wilde

17:42 The easiest way to give up smoking is to stop putting cigarettes in your mouth and lighting them.

William Rushton

17:43   I always pass on good advice – it's the only thing one can do with it.

Oscar Wilde

17:44   From the silence that prevails I conclude that Lauderdale has been telling a joke.

Richard Brinsley Sheridan

17:45   First left, go along the corridor. You'll see a door marked Gentlemen, but don't let that deter you.

F.E. Smith

17:46   It is very easy to endure the difficulties of one's enemies. It is the successes of one's friends that are hard to bear.

Oscar Wilde

17:47   The cocktail party – as the name itself indicates – was originally invented by dogs. They are simply bottom-sniffings raised to the rank of formal ceremonies.

Lawrence Durrell

17:48   This year Elizabeth Taylor is wearing Orson Welles designer jeans.

Joan Rivers

17:49   Frank Harris has been invited to every great house in England – once.

Oscar Wilde

17:50   Here's a rule I recommend. Never practise two vices at once.

Tallulah Bankhead

17:51   I can resist everything except temptation.

Oscar Wilde

17:52   There is not a single person between the ages of fifteen and twenty-five in the whole of Bicester or Welwyn Garden City who does not have to be woken every morning with stimulants in order that he may drift through the day on sedatives.

Quentin Crisp

17:53   Fashion is a form of ugliness so intolerable that we have to alter it every six months.

Oscar Wilde

17:54   I've had a wonderful evening – but this wasn't it.

Groucho Marx

17:55 You should study the Peerage; it is the best thing in fiction the English have ever done.

Oscar Wilde

17:56 I live in terror of not being misunderstood.

Oscar Wilde

17:57 If you can keep your head when all about you are losing theirs, it is possible you haven't grasped the gravity of the situation.

Jean Kerr

17:58 A careful driver is one who looks in both directions when he passes a red light.

Ralph Marterie

17:59 The extraordinary thing about the lower classes in England is that they are always losing their relations. They are extremely fortunate in that respect.

Oscar Wilde

17:60 Fate bestowed on M. Genet certain special advantages. He was illegitimate and spent his childhood in an orphanage. From there he graduated to a reformatory.

Quentin Crisp

17:61 If you don't go to other men's funerals, they won't go to yours.

Clarence S. Day

17:62 Giving up smoking is the easiest thing in the world. I know because I've done it thousands of times.

Mark Twain

17:63 Whoever thinks of going to bed before twelve o'clock is a scoundrel.

Samuel Johnson

17:64 Don't forget to tell everyone it's a secret.

Gerald F. Lieberman

17:65 I don't care to belong to any club that will accept me as a member.

Groucho Marx

17:66 I have often envied Gerry Wellesley the faculty of giving people rapid and often accurate information.

Harold Nicolson

17:67 The English country gentleman galloping after a fox – the unspeakable in full pursuit of the uneatable.

Oscar Wilde

17:68 Every normal man must be tempted, at times, to spit on his hands, hoist the black flag, and begin slitting throats.

H.L. Mencken

17:69 I'd rather eat shit than wear a suit.

Billy Carter

17:70 Some people can stay longer in an hour than others can in a week.

William D. Howells

17:71 Never rub bottoms with a porcupine.

Jane Philbin

17:72 Never in the history of fashion has so little material been raised so high to reveal so much that needs to be covered so badly.

Cecil Beaton

17:73 All the things I really like are either immoral, illegal or fattening.

Alexander Woollcott

17:74 The perfect hostess will see to it that books written by male and female authors be properly separated on her book-shelves. Their proximity, unless they happen to be married, should not be tolerated.

Lady Gough

17:75 The Mediterranean? Not any more, dear. It's the Elsan of Europe.

Alan Bennett

17:76 I'm glad to hear you smoke. A man should always have an occupation of some kind. There are far too many idle men in London as it is.

Oscar Wilde

17:77 You can get much further with a kind word and a gun than you can with a kind word alone.

Al Capone

17:78 I'd hate to drown. You look so awful afterwards.

Alan Ayckbourn

17:79 American women expect to find in their husbands a perfection that English women only hope to find in their butlers.

Somerset Maugham

17:80 We were so poor we didn't even have a lavatory brush. We used to tie my pet hedgehog to a stick and tell him to hold his breath.

Roy Brown

17:81 Sexual fidelity is not necessary to a well-conducted marriage. Your eldest son should certainly be your own, but beyond this it is excessively vulgar to enquire too closely into the paternity of your children.

Simon Raven

17:82 My brother has an unusual job – he finds things before other people lose them.

Frank Carson

17:83 I don't mind your smoking, if you don't mind my being sick all over you.

Thomas Beecham

17:84 When women kiss, it always reminds me of prize-fighters shaking hands.

H.L. Mencken

17:85 Kensington Gardens has been annexed as a middle-class rendezvous, and good society no longer goes there except to drown itself.

Princess Lieven

17:86 It is a fact that not once in my life have I gone out for a walk. I have been taken out for walks; but that is another matter.

Max Beerbohm

17:87 Anybody who has to ask what is the upkeep of a yacht cannot afford one.

J.P. Morgan

17:88 Why should we tolerate the system where a man with an amputated leg must get a medical certificate to state that the leg had not regrown each time he wants his allowances renewed?

Franklin Bicknell

17:89 Hypocrisy is the Vaseline of social intercourse.

J.R. Newman

17:90 I attribute my long and healthy life to the fact that I never touched a cigarette, a drink, or a girl until I was ten years old.

George Moore

17:91 To avoid lunatics on buses, sit in the middle of the bus. The friendly lunatics sit as close to the driver as they can, and the unfriendly ones sit as far away as they can.

Keith Allan Hunter

17:92 If you wait long enough beside the river you will see the bodies of your enemies float by.

Ying Chu

17:93 The true test is not whether a man behaves like a gentleman, but whether he misbehaves like one.

Sydney Tremayne

17:94 To every human problem there is a neat and easy solution – and it's wrong.

H.L. Mencken

17:95 A cigarette is the perfect type of a perfect pleasure. It is exquisite and leaves one quite unsatisfied. What more can one want?

Oscar Wilde

17:96 I wish I loved the human race;
I wish I loved its silly face;
I wish I liked the way it walks;
I wish I liked the way it talks;
And when I'm introduced to one
I wish I thought, What jolly fun.

Walter Raleigh

17:97 Blessed is he who expects no gratitude, for he shall not be disappointed.

W.C. Bennett

17:98 I was always unlawful; I broke the law when I was born because my parents weren't married.

George Bernard Shaw

17:99 Twenty-two acknowledged concubines and a library of sixty-two thousand volumes, attested the variety of the inclinations of the Emperor Gordian, and from the productions which he left behind him, it appears that the former as well as the latter were designed for use rather than ostentation.

Edward Gibbon

17:100 He was the sort of man who would throw a drowning man both ends of a rope.

Arthur Baer

17:101 You can measure the social caste of a person by the distance between the husband's and wife's apartments.

King Alfonso XIII

17:102 Every luxury was lavished on you – atheism, breastfeeding, circumcision.

Joe Orton

17:103 I think that black people should be given a fair crack of the whip.

Margaret Thatcher

17:104 Arson is not really a crime. There are many buildings that deserve to be burned down.

H.G. Wells

17:105 Always choose the oldest customs' official. No chance of promotion.

Somerset Maugham

17:106 Capital punishment is our society's recognition of the sanctity of human life.

Orrin Hatch

17:107 I much prefer travelling in non-British ships. There's none of that nonsense about women and children first.

Somerset Maugham

17:108 This is a free country. Folks have the right to send me letters, and I have the right not to open them.

William Faulkner

17:109 For parlour use the vague generality is a life-saver.

George Ade

17:110 To succeed in life it is not enough to be stupid. One must be well mannered as well.

Bonar Thompson

17:111 Mr Frick is the only man I know whom Dale Carnegie would have hit in the mouth.

Bill Veech

17:112 It was such a lovely day I thought it was a pity to get up.
Somerset Maugham

17:113 Yea, though I should walk through the valley of the shadow of death, I shall fear no evil, because I am the meanest son-of-a-bitch in the valley.

Gene M. Nordby

17:114 The great thing about suicide is that it's not one of those things you have to do now or lose your chance. You can always do it later.

Harvey Fierstein

17:115 Start off every day with a smile and get it over with.
W.C. Fields

17:116 Thirty-five is a very attractive age. London society is full of women who have of their own free choice remained thirty-five for years.

Oscar Wilde

17:117 You really have to get to know Dewey to dislike him.
Robert A. Taft

17:118 I should like one of these days to be so well known, so popular, so celebrated, so famous, that it would permit me to break wind in society and society would think it a most natural thing.

Honoré De Balzac

17:119 The members of the Aesthetic Movement between the wars spent on sodomy what they got by sponging.

George Orwell

17:120 I like long walks, especially when they are taken by people who annoy me.

Noel Coward

17:121 Half the world does not know how the other half lives, but is trying to find out.

Edgar W. Howe

17:122 I am in no need of your God damned sympathy. I ask only to be entertained by some of your grosser reminiscences.

Alexander Woollcott

17:123 Don't misunderstand me – my dislike for her is purely platonic.

Herbert Beerbohm Tree

17:124 At superior nudist camps, a nice class distinction was made; the butlers and maids who brought along the refreshments were forced to admit their lower social standing by wearing loincloths and aprons respectively.

Robert Graves

17:125 Never support two weaknesses at a time. It's your combination sinners – your lecherous liars and your miserly drunkards – who dishonour the vices and bring them into bad repute.

Thornton Wilder

17:126 When I want a peerage, I shall buy one like an honest man.

Lord Northcliffe

17:127 I have always regarded the telling of funny stories as the last refuge of the witless, the supreme consolation of dirty minded commercial travellers, wrenched from their homes and wireless sets.

Nathaniel Gubbins

17:128 The man who has cured himself of B.O. and halitosis, has learned French to surprise the waiter, and the saxophone to amuse the company, may find that people still avoid him because they do not like him.

Heywood Broun

17:129 The lie is the basic building block of good manners.

Quentin Crisp

17:130 No one really listens to anyone else, and if you try it for a while you will see why.

Mignon McLaughlin

17:131 To qualify as a member of the Women's Royal Voluntary Service you need to be able to wear a cardigan and jumper and a rope of pearls and to have had a hysterectomy.

Stella Reading

17:132 A bore is a man who when you ask him how he is, tells you.

B.L. Taylor

17:133 For seventeen years, George the Fifth did nothing at all but kill animals and stick in stamps.

Harold Nicholson

17:134 Because of the war shortages, there will be no napkins at dinner tonight. Instead, from time to time a woolly dog will pass among you.

Oscar Levant

17:135 The best indicator of a man's honesty isn't his income tax return. It's the zero adjustment on his bathroom scales.

Arthur C. Clarke

17:136 Beware of the conversationalist who adds 'in conclusion'. He is merely starting afresh.

Robert Morley

17:137 When I found a gibbet in an unexplored part of Africa, the sight of it gave me infinite pleasure, as it proved I was in a civilised society.

Mungo Park

17:138 If you think before you speak, the other fellow gets his joke in first.

Edgar W. Howe

17:139 'I believe I take precedence,' he said coldly; 'you are merely the club bore: I am the club liar.'

H.H. Munro

17:140 I loathe people who keep dogs. They are cowards who haven't the guts to bite people themselves.

August Strindberg

17:141 A healthy male adult bore consumes each year one and a half times his own weight in other people's patience.

John Updike

17:142 When the war broke out she took down the signed photograph of the Kaiser and, with some solemnity, hung it in the menservants' lavatory; it was her one combative action.

Evelyn Waugh

17:143 An interpreter is one who enables two persons of different languages to understand each other by repeating to each what it would have been to the interpreter's advantage for the other to have said.

Ambrose Bierce

17:144 It was said of Sarah, Duchess of Marlborough, that she never put dots over her i's, to save ink.

Horace Walpole

17:145 It's going to be fun to watch and see how long the meek can keep the earth after they inherit it.

Kin Hubbard

17:146 I like to visit my friends from time to time just to look over my library.

William Hazlitt

17:147 I see that the President of Rumania's mother is dead – there's always trouble for somebody.

Alan Bennett

17:148 I didn't have 3,000 pairs of shoes. I had only 1,060 pairs.

Imelda Marcos

Sport

18:1 Football is all very well a good game for rough girls, but not for delicate boys.

Oscar Wilde

18:2 Much as bookmakers are opposed to law-breaking they are not bigoted about it.

Damon Runyon

18:3 When Nicklaus plays well he wins; when he plays badly he comes second. When he plays terribly he's third.

Johnny Miller

18:4 If there is a thunderstorm on a golf course, walk down the middle of the fairway holding a one-iron over your head. Even God can't hit a one-iron.

Lee Trevino

18:5 He hit me among my face.

Henny Youngman

18:6 If the people don't want to come out to the ball park, nobody's gonna stop 'em.

Yogi Berra

18:7 There are fools, damn fools, and jockeys who remount in a steeplechase.

John Oaksey

18:8 This city has two great football teams – Liverpool and Liverpool reserves.

Bill Shankly

18:9 I've seen better swings than Bob Hope's in a condemned playground.

Arnold Palmer

18:10 Of course I have played outdoor games. I once played dominoes in an open air cafe in Paris.

Oscar Wilde

18:11 Never play cards with a man named Doc.

Nelson Algren

18:12 Some people think football is a matter of life and death. I don't like that attitude. I can assure them it is much more serious than that.

Bill Shankly

18:13 Women playing cricket should treat it as a matter between consenting females in private.

Michael Parkinson

18:14 Go jogging? What, and get hit by a meteor?

Robert Benchley

18:15 My grandfather couldn't prescribe a pill to make a greyhound run faster, but he could produce one to make the other five go slower.

Benny Green

18:16 When I got into the boxing ring women used to scream with delight because usually I'd left my shorts in the locker.

Roy Brown

18:17 That's what I call an airport shot. You hit one of those, you miss the cut and you're heading off for the airport.

Lee Trevino

18:18 The hardest thing about boxing is picking up your teeth with a boxing glove on.

Kin Hubbard

18:19 Anybody can win, unless there happens to be a second entry.

George Ade

18:20 The only exercise I ever get is taking the cuff-links out of one shirt and putting them in another.

Ring Lardner

18:21 Trust everybody – but cut the cards.

Finley Peter Dunne

18:22 You don't know what pressure is in golf until you play for five bucks with only two in your pocket.

Lee Trevino

18:23 Wales didn't even have enough imagination to thump someone in the line-out when the ref wasn't looking.

J.P.R. Williams

18:24 It is frequently asserted in bookmaking circles that my mother and father met only once and then for a very brief period.

Lord Wigg

18:25 Although he is a bad fielder, he is also a very poor hitter.

Ring Lardner

18:26 I have hunted deer on occasions, but they were not aware of it.

Felix Gear

18:27 The rules of soccer are basically simple – if it moves, kick it; if it doesn't move, kick it until it does.

Phil Woosnam

18:28 I failed to make the chess team because of my height.

Woody Allen

18:29 Losing the Super Bowl is worse than death. With death you don't have to get up next morning.

George Allen

18:30 A fishing rod is a stick with a worm at one end and a fool at the other.

Samuel Johnson

18:31 A proper definition of an amateur sportsman today is one who accepts cash, not cheques.

Jack Kelly

18:32 Life is just an elaborate metaphor for cricket.

Marvin Cohen

18:33 I cannot see who is leading in the Boat Race, but it's either Oxford or Cambridge.

John Snagge

18:34 I should like to be a horse.

Elizabeth Windsor

18:35 I went to a fight the other night and a hockey game broke out.

Rodney Dangerfield

18:36 The race is not always to the swift, nor the battle to the strong – but that's the way to bet.

Damon Runyon

18:37 I want to thank all the people who made this meeting necessary.

Yogi Berra

18:38 Never play tennis for money against a grey-haired player.

Tom Robinson

18:39 When I was a coach at Rochester they called me in and said 'We're making a change in your department'. I was the only guy in my department.

Don Cherry

18:40 Footballers are miry gladiators whose sole purpose in life is to position a surrogate human head between two poles.

Elizabeth Hogg

18:41 Winning isn't everything – it's the only thing.

Vince Lombardi

18:42 There is plenty of time to win this game, and to trash the Spaniards too – my bowels cannot wait.

Francis Drake

18:43 My horse was in the lead, coming down the home stretch, but the caddie fell off.

Samuel Goldwyn

18:44 Herbert Strudwick used to recommend to wicket-keepers 'Rinse your hands in the chamber pot every day. The urine hardens them wonderfully'.

David Lemmon

18:45 Skiing combines outdoor fun with knocking down trees with your face.

Dave Barry

18:46 You can observe a lot just by watching.

Yogi Berra

18:47 If you want a track team to win the high jump, you find one person who can jump seven feet, not seven people who can each jump one foot.

Frederick E. Terman

18:48 I'd give my right arm to get back into the England team.

Peter Shilton

18:49 Remember, postcards only, please. The winner will be the first one opened.

Brian Moore

18:50 A computer once beat me at chess, but it was no match for me at kick boxing.

Emo Philips

18:51 The British Board of Censors will not pass any seduction scene unless the seducer has one foot on the floor. Apparently sex in England is something like snooker.

Fred Allen

18:52 What a terrible round. I only hit two good balls all day and that was when I stepped on a rake in a bunker.

Lee Trevino

18:53 Pro basketball coaching is when you wake up in the morning and wish your parents had never met.

Bill Fitch

18:54 Remember, it doesn't matter whether you win or lose; what matters is whether I win or lose.

Darrin Weinberg

18:55 I'm going to win so much money this year that my caddie will make the top twenty money-winners list.

Lee Trevino

18:56 I'd like to borrow Muhammad Ali's body for just forty-eight hours. There are three guys I'd like to beat up and four women I'd like to make love to.

Jim Murray

18:57 You can have sex either before cricket or after cricket – the fundamental fact is that cricket must be there at the centre of things.

Harold Pinter

18:58 If at first you don't succeed – so much for skydiving.

Henny Youngman

18:59 I resigned as coach because of illness and fatigue. The fans were sick and tired of me.

John Ralston

18:60 Football combines the worst features of American life – frantic violence punctuated by committee meetings.

George Will

18:61 Grouse shooting begins on August 12th. A grouse shot before that date tends to be very annoyed.

Michael Shea

18:62 We should be thankful to lynch mobs. I've got a brother who can run a half mile faster than any white boy in the world.

Dick Gregory

18:63 A sportsman is a man who, every now and then, simply has to get out and kill something.

Stephen Leacock

18:64 Look laddie, if you're in the penalty area and aren't quite sure what to do with the ball, just stick it in the net and we'll discuss all your options afterwards.

Bill Shankly

18:65 The athletic facilities situation is a mess. Girls still haven't figured out how to use the urinals.

John Roberts

18:66 Of course there should be women basketball referees. Incompetence should not be confined to one sex.

Bill Russell

18:67 When Nastase is winning, he's objectionable. When he's losing, he's highly objectionable.

Adrian Clark

18:68 I'll fine any of my players who wins the Lady Byng Trophy for ice hockey gentlemanly conduct.

Punch Imlach

18:69 There are few tactical rules for mixed doubles. One is to hit the girl whenever possible.

Bill Tilden

18:70 Anyone who burns a cross on my lawn, he won't burn anything ever again if I catch him.

Sonny Liston

18:71 My golfing partner couldn't hit a tiled floor with a bellyful of puke.

David Feherty

18:72 Give me my golf clubs, fresh air and a beautiful partner, and you can keep my golf clubs and the fresh air.

Jack Benny

18:73 Monica Seles – I'd hate to be next door to her on her wedding night.

Peter Ustinov

18:74 I've seen George Foreman shadow boxing and the shadow won.

Muhammad Ali

18:75 In the World Darts Championships in 1982, Jocky Wilson missed when attempting to shake hands with an opponent.

Craig Brown

18:76 Golf is an ineffectual attempt to direct an uncontrollable sphere into an inaccessible hole with instruments ill-adapted to the purpose.

Winston Churchill

18:77 W.G. Grace had one of the dirtiest necks I ever kept wicket behind.

George Cobham

18:78 I am to cricket what Dame Sybil Thorndyke is to nonferrous welding.

Frank Muir

18:79 Never catch a loose horse. You could end up all day holding the f•••••• thing.

Lester Piggott

18:80 Golf is so popular simply because it is the best game in the world at which to be bad.

A.A. Milne

18:81 She leads away from aces and neglects to keep my jump bids alive. But she is still my mother.

Heywood Broun

18:82 Professional wrestling's most mystifying hold is on its audience.

Luke Neely

18:83 Moving from Wales to Italy is like going to a different country.

Ian Rush

18:84 I love Liverpool so much that if I caught one of their players in bed with my missus I'd tiptoe downstairs and make him a cup of tea.

A. Koppite

18:85 If I had to choose between sex and snooker, I'd choose snooker.

Steve Davis

18:86 I have a bad swing, a bad stance and a bad grip, but my bank manager loves me.

Lee Trevino

18:87 Perhaps if I dyed my hair peroxide blond and called myself the great white tadpole, that would help.

Ian Woosnam

18:88 One should always play fairly when one has the winning cards.

Oscar Wilde

18:89 I object to hare coursing on the grounds that *real* men should tear the live hares apart with their own teeth. Why should the dogs have all the fun?

Ernest Hemingway

18:90 The man who caught that fish is a liar.

George Robey

18:91 I don't like money, actually, but I find it quiets my nerves.

Joe Louis

18:92 The amateur rugby union player has an inalienable right to play like a pillock.

Dick Greenwood

18:93 The trouble with referees is that they just don't care which side wins.

Tom Canterbury

18:94 I am not my brother's wicketkeeper.

Clyde Packer

18:95 People started calling me 'Fiery' because 'Fiery' rhymes with 'Fred' just like 'Typhoon' rhymes with 'Tyson'.

Fred Trueman

18:96 With good practice at high level diving you can avoid killing yourself.

Elizabeth MacKay

18:97 If me and King Kong went into an alley, only one of us would come out. And it wouldn't be the monkey.

Lyle Alzado

18:98 Al Davis is a very smart man. He's probably the only one who knows the serial number of the Unknown Soldier.

Sam Rutigliano

18:99 I've never seen such skinny legs on a football player before. I wonder if he ever caught the rustler who stole his calves?

Steve Jordan

18:100 In running you have to be suspicious when you line up against girls with moustaches.

Maree Holland

18:101 Anyone who doesn't watch rugby league is not a real person. He's a cow's hoof, an ethnic, senile or comes from Melbourne.

John Singleton

18:102 Modern rugby players like to get their retaliation in first.

Kim Fletcher

18:103 If a lot of people gripped a knife and fork like they do a golf club, they'd starve to death.

Sam Snead

18:104 Boxing is a lot of white men watching two black men beat each other up.

Muhammad Ali

18:105 Golf is like an eighteen-year-old girl with big boobs. You know it's wrong but you can't keep away from her.

Val Doonican

18:106 Rugby is a ruffian's game played by gentlemen; soccer is a gentlemen's game played by ruffians; and Gaelic football is a ruffian's game played by ruffians.

Patrick Murray

18:107 The first time I saw Walter Payton in the locker room, I thought, God must have taken a hammer and said to Himself, 'I'm going to make me a half-back'.

Fred O'Connor

18:108 Skiing? Why should I break my leg at forty degrees below zero when I can fall downstairs at home?

Corey Ford

18:109 The Gullikson twins, Tim and Tom, are both from Wisconsin.

Dan Maskell

18:110 I saw Joe Di Maggio last night and he wasn't wearing his baseball suit. This struck me as rather foolish. Suppose a ball game broke out in the middle of the night? By the time he got into his suit the game would be over.

Groucho Marx

18:111 It took me seventeen years to get three thousand hits in baseball. I did it in one afternoon on the golf course.

Henry Aaron

18:112 What they say about footballers being ignorant is rubbish. I spoke to a couple yesterday and they were quite intelligent.

Raquel Welch

18:113 Fate was kind to him, dealing him a hand of five aces.

Harry Wilson

18:114 Being a manager is simple. All you have to do is to keep the five players who hate your guts away from the five who are undecided.

Casey Stengel

18:115 I see two fellows in the ring; I hit the one that isn't there and the one that is there hits me.

Billy Softly

18:116 I am donating a shilling to W.G. Grace's testimonial not in support of cricket, but as an earnest protest against golf.

Max Beerbohm

18:117 Last time we got a penalty away from home, Christ was still a carpenter.

Lennie Lawrence

18:118 A bookie is just a pickpocket who lets you use your own hands.

Henry Morgan

18:119 Yes we've had bad times at Anfield; one year we came second.

Bob Paisley

18:120 I refuse to play golf with Errol Flynn. If I want to play with a prick, I'll play with my own.

W.C. Fields

18:121 Baseball is very big with my people. It's the only time we can get to shake a bat at a white man without starting a riot.

Dick Gregory

18:122 If you ever get belted and see three fighters through a haze, go after the one in the middle. That's what ruined me – I went after the two guys on the end.

Max Baer

18:123 If Stan Bowles could pass a betting shop like he can pass a football, he'd have no worries at all.

Ernie Tagg

18:124 I shall continue to give relegated Luton my full support – in fact I'm wearing it at this very moment.

Eric Morecambe

18:125 Now that I have won the Olympic heavyweight weight-lifting gold medal, maybe my wife will show more respect.

Vasily Alexeyev

18:126 I have seen players, famous internationals, in an airport lounge all get up and follow one bloke to the toilet. Six of them maybe, all standing there not wanting a piss themselves, but following the bloke who does.

Geoff Hurst

18:127 My definition of a foreigner is someone who doesn't understand cricket.

Anthony Couch

18:128 Gary Lineker is the Queen Mother of football.

James Christopher

18:129 I never play cricket. It requires one to assume such indecent postures.

Oscar Wilde

18:130 All rowed fast, but none so fast as stroke.

Desmond Coke

18:131 The only reason I would take up jogging is so I could hear heavy breathing again.

Erma Bombeck

Theatre and Criticism

19:1 I have knocked everything in this play except the chorus girls' knees, and there God anticipated me.
Percy Hammond

19:2 If laughter is contagious, my son has found the cure.
Les Dawson's Mother

19:3 You wouldn't get away with that if my script writer was here.
Bob Hope

19:4 I saw the play under adverse conditions – the curtain was up.
Robert Benchley

19:5 If there are any of you at the back who do not hear me, there is no use raising your hands because I am also near-sighted.
W.H. Auden

19:6 Chevy Chase couldn't ad-lib a fart after a baked bean dinner.
Johnny Carson

19:7 A first night audience consists of the unburied dead.
Orson Bean

19:8 Critics are like eunuchs in a harem; they know exactly how it should be done – they see it being done every night, but they can't do it themselves.
Brendan Behan

19:9 *Waiting For Godot* is a play in which nothing happens, twice.
Vivian Mercier

19:10 The impact of the play was like the banging together of two damp dish-cloths.
Brendan Behan

19:11 Two things in the play should have been cut. The second act and that youngster's throat.
Noel Coward

19:12 My agent gets ten per cent of everything I get, except the blinding headaches.

Fred Allen

19:13 The play was a great success, but the audience was a disaster.

Oscar Wilde

19:14 No one can have a higher opinion of him than I have – and I think he is a dirty little beast.

W.S. Gilbert

19:15 There is absolutely nothing wrong with Oscar Levant that a miracle cannot fix.

Alexander Woollcott

19:16 The central problem in *Hamlet* is whether the critics are mad or only pretending to be mad.

Oscar Wilde

19:17 He played the King as if he was afraid that at any moment someone would play the ace.

Eugene Field

19:18 Robert Mitchum does not so much act as point his suit at people.

Russell Davies

19:19 Go on writing plays my boy. One of these days a London producer will go into his office and say to his secretary, 'Is there a play from Shaw this morning?' and when she says 'No', he will say, 'Well, then we'll have to start on the rubbish'. And that's your chance my boy.

George Bernard Shaw

19:20 Asking a writer what he thinks about critics is like asking a lamp-post what it thinks about dogs.

John Osborne

19:21 I like work; it fascinates me. I can sit and look at it for hours.

Jerome K. Jerome

19:22 Comedy, like sodomy, is an unnatural act.

Marty Feldman

19:23 There is less in this play than meets the eye.

Tallulah Bankhead

19:24 What is *Uncle Vanya* about? I would say it is about as much as I can take.

Roger Garland

19:25 I can take any amount of criticism, so long as it is unqualified praise.

Noel Coward

19:26 What is the play about? It's about to make me a great deal of money.

Tom Stoppard

19:27 I go to the theatre to be entertained. I don't want to see rape, sodomy, incest and drug addiction. I can get all of that at home.

Peter Cook

19:28 Liza Minelli comes out looking like a giant rodent en route to a costume ball.

Stanley Kauffmann

19:29 Critics are pygmies with poison darts who live in the valley of the sleeping giants.

Dagobert D. Runes

19:30 My reputation grows with every failure.

George Bernard Shaw

19:31 One of the first and most important things for a critic to learn is how to sleep undetected at the theatre.

William Archer

19:32 They are going to dig up Shakespeare and dig up Bacon; they are going to get Beerbohm Tree to recite *Hamlet* to them, and the one who turns in his coffin will be the author of the play.

W.S. Gilbert

19:33 The secret of my great talent as an actor is that I speak in a loud clear voice and try not to bump into the furniture.

Alfred Lunt

19:34 An actress is someone with no ability who sits around waiting to go on alimony.

Jackie Stallone

19:35 One of my chief regrets during my years in the theatre is that I couldn't sit in the audience and watch myself.

John Barrymore

19:36 Actresses are another kettle of bitch.

Gilbert Harding

19:37 Scratch an actor – and you'll find an actress.

Dorothy Parker

19:38 In England nobody goes to the theatre unless he or she has bronchitis.

James Agate

19:39 A fan club is a group of people who tell an actor that he is not alone in the way he feels about himself.

Jack Carson

19:40 Some of the greatest love affairs I have known involved one actor, unassisted.

Wilson Mizner

19:41 Sarah Bernhardt is a great actress from the waist down.

Margaret Kendal

19:42 The scenery was beautiful – but the actors got in front of it.

Alexander Woollcott

19:43 *O Calcutta* is the sort of show that gives pornography a bad name.

Clive Barnes

19:44 My dear sir, I have read your play. Oh, my dear sir.

Herbert Beerbohm Tree

19:45 Depending upon shock tactics is easy, whereas writing a good play is difficult. Pubic hair is no substitute for wit.

J.B. Priestley

19:46 Richard Burton as Caliban looked like a miner with a tail coming up from a coal face.

James Agate

19:47 The plot of *Who Killed Agatha Christie* has as many holes as a sieve and is far less entertaining.

Bernard Levin

19:48 If she were cast as Lady Godiva, the horse would steal the show.

Patrick Murray

19:49 Sarah Brightman couldn't act scared on the New York subway at four o'clock in the morning.

Joel Segal

19:50 Only one joke of *Rose Marie* was applauded: 'We are all going into the fitting room to have a fit.' This kind of brilliance was not sustained.

Clive Barnes

19:51 In Tyrone Guthrie's production of *Hamlet*, Mr Frederick Bennett's first gravedigger is the one gloomy spot in the entire production.

James Agate

19:52 Richard Briers last night played *Hamlet* like a demented typewriter.

W.A. Darlington

19:53 Stephen Fry has all the wit of an unflushed toilet.

Bernard Manning

19:54 Peter O'Toole delivers every line with a monotonous tenor bark as if addressing an audience of deaf Eskimos.

Michael Billington

19:55 The play left a taste of lukewarm parsnip juice.

Alexander Woollcott

19:56 A star is anyone who has shaken hands with Lew Grade, and a superstar is someone who has refused to shake hands with Lew Grade.

Harry Secombe

19:57 Elizabeth Taylor – just how garish her commonplace accent, her squeakily shrill voice, and the childish petulance with which she delivers her lines are, my pen is neither scratchy nor leaky enough to convey.

John Simon

19:58 Edith Sitwell is like a high altar on the move.

Elizabeth Bowen

19:59   He wanted to be an actor. He had all the qualifications, including no money and a total lack of responsibility.

Hedda Hopper

19:60   I don't believe in dying. It's been done. I'm working on a new exit. Besides, I can't die now – I'm booked.

George Burns

19:61   A plagiarist is a writer of plays.

Oscar Wilde

Miscellaneous

20:1　The realisation that one is to be hanged in the morning concentrates the mind wonderfully.

Samuel Johnson

20:2　There is only one way to find out if a man is honest – ask him. If he says 'yes' he's not honest.

Groucho Marx

20:3　Never kick a fresh turd on a hot day.

Harry S. Truman

20:4　The kilt is an unrivalled garment for fornication and diarrhoea.

John Masters

20:5　A filing cabinet is a place where you can lose things systematically.

T. H. Thompson

20:6　The snowdrop is more powerful than the Panzer.

Beverley Nichols

20:7　Princess Anne is such an active lass. So outdoorsy. She loves nature in spite of what nature did to her.

Bette Midler

20:8　It is always the best policy to tell the truth, unless of course you happen to be an exceptionally good liar.

Jerome K. Jerome

20:9　The reports of my death have been greatly exaggerated.

Mark Twain

20:10　One morning I shot an elephant in my pyjamas. How he got in my pyjamas I'll never know.

Groucho Marx

20:11　I know the answer! The answer lies within the heart of mankind! The answer is twelve? I must be in the wrong book.

Charles Schultz

20:12 Summer has set in with its usual severity.

S.T. Coleridge

20:13 See the happy moron, he doesn't give a damn. I wish I were a moron: my God, perhaps I am.

R. Fairchild

20:14 Rumpers was a little man. He made no secret of his height.

Alan Bennett

20:15 Just how big a coward am I? Well I was on the Olympic team.

Bob Hope

20:16 I have too much respect for the truth then to drag it out on every trifling occasion.

Mark Twain

20:17 Always look out for number one and be careful not to step in number two.

Rodney Dangerfield

20:18 Too intense contemplation of his own genius had begun to undermine his health.

Max Beerbohm

20:19 I used to sell furniture for a living. The trouble was, it was my own.

Les Dawson

20:20 I'm not afraid of heights but I'm afraid of widths.

Steven Wright

20:21 There is nothing safer than flying – it's crashing that is dangerous.

Theo Cowan

20:22 One, two, three
Buckle my shoe.

Robert Benchley

20:23 A pedestrian is anyone who is knocked down by a motor car.

J.B. Morton

20:24 I never forget a face, but in your case I'm willing to make an exception.

Groucho Marx

20:25 One should try everything once, except incest and folk-dancing.

Arnold Bax

20:26 The trouble with this country is that there are too many people going about saying 'The trouble with this country is ...'

Sinclair Lewis

20:27 If dirt was trumps, what a hand you would hold!

Charles Lamb

20:28 I resigned from the army after two weeks service in the field, explaining I was 'incapacitated by fatigue' through persistent retreating.

Mark Twain

20:29 A committee is a cul-de-sac into which ideas are lured and then quietly strangled.

John A. Lincoln

20:30 On a Polar expedition begin with a clear idea which Pole you are aiming at, and try to start facing the right way. Choose your companions carefully – you may have to eat them.

W.C. Sellar

20:31 Go, and never darken my towels again.

Groucho Marx

20:32 The toilet paper was composed of quartered sheets of typing paper, with holes in one corner. These were covered in messages, many of them marked 'Secret' and some of them marked 'Top Secret'.

Peter Ustinov

20:33 The human race, to which so many of my readers belong ...

G.K. Chesterton

20:34 The dog was licking its private parts with the gusto of an alderman drinking soup.

Graham Greene

20:35 Such time as he can spare from the adornment of his person he devotes to the neglect of his duties.

Samuel Johnson

20:36. Always remember the poor – it costs nothing.

Josh Billings

20:37 'I'm very brave generally,' he went on in a low voice: 'only today I happen to have a headache.'

Lewis Carroll

20:38 No problem is insoluble, given a big enough plastic bag.

Tom Stoppard

20:39 Death is psychosomatic.

Charles Manson

20:40 I had a terrific idea this morning but I didn't like it.

Samuel Goldwyn

20:41 Self-decapitation is an extremely difficult, not to say dangerous thing to attempt.

W.S. Gilbert

20:42 I don't know what effect these men will have upon the enemy, but, by God, they terrify me.

Duke of Wellington

20:43 The most hazardous part of our expedition to Africa was crossing Piccadilly Circus.

Joseph Thomson

20:44 I admire Cecil Rhodes, I frankly confess it; and when the time comes I shall buy a piece of the rope for a keepsake.

Mark Twain

20:45 The biggest fool in the world hasn't been born yet.

Josh Billings

20:46 Guy Burgess had the look of an inquisitive rodent emerging into daylight from a drain.

Harold Nicolson

20:47 A large body of men have expressed their willingness to serve in the Army against Napoleon subject to the condition that they should not be sent overseas – except I presume in case of invasion.

William Pitt

20:48 What happens to the holes when the Swiss cheese is eaten?

Bertolt Brecht

20:49 The lion and the calf shall lie down together but the calf won't get much sleep.

Woody Allen

20:50 Another victory like that and we are done for.

Pyrrhus

20:51 I have bad reflexes. I was once run over by a car being pushed by two guys.

Woody Allen

20:52 I can believe anything as long as it is incredible.

Oscar Wilde

20:53 The man who would stoop so low as to write an anonymous letter, the least he might do is to sign his name to it.

Boyle Roach

20:54 A man cannot be in two places at the same time unless he is a bird.

Boyle Roach

20:55 'I will only shake my finger at him,' he said, and placed it on the trigger.

Stanislaw J. Lec

20:56 No man is an island but some of us are pretty long peninsulas.

Ashleigh Brilliant

20:57 Underground we have coal for 600 years. Above it we have Mr Shinwell. Reversal of these positions would solve our present troubles.

R.A. Whitsun

20:58 According to the Law of the West, a Colt 45 beats four aces.

Bill Jones

20:59 As I hurtled through space, one thought kept crossing my mind – every part of this capsule was supplied by the lowest bidder.

John Glynn

20:60 Kindly inform troops immediately that all communications have broken down.

Ashleigh Brilliant

20:61 There are two classes of people in the world – those who divide people into two classes and those who don't.

Robert Benchley

20:62 If you think the problem is bad now, just wait until we've solved it.

Arthur Kasspe

20:63 Dogs are sons of bitches.

W.C. Fields

20:64 I was brought up to respect my elders so now I don't have to respect anybody.

George Burns

20:65 I haven't killed anyone all day – help me keep it that way.

Clint Eastwood

20:66 What smells so? Has somebody been burning a rag or is there a dead mule in the back yard? No, the man is smoking a five-cent cigar.

Eugene Field

20:67 You can have an affection for a murderer or a sodomite, but you cannot have an affection for a man whose breath stinks.

George Orwell

20:68 In the space age, man will be able to go around the world in two hours – one hour for flying and the other to get to the airport.

Neil M. McElroy

20:69 Don't stand around doing nothing – people will think you're just a workman.

Spike Milligan

20:70 Cleopatra had the body of a roll-top desk and the mind of a duck.

Rowan Atkinson

20:71 If everyone minded their own business, the world would go round a great deal faster than it does.

Lewis Carroll

20:72 It may be December outside, ladies, but under your armpits, it is always August.

John Snagge

20:73 To write a diary every day is like returning to one's own vomit.

Enoch Powell

20:74 A Coarse Sailor is one who in a crisis forgets nautical language and shouts, 'For God's sake turn left'.

Michael Green

20:75 Many a man who can't direct you to a corner drugstore will get a respectful hearing when age has further impaired his mind.

Finley Peter Dunne

20:76 It is not enough to succeed – others must fail.

Gore Vidal

20:77 Yesterday was the first day of the rest of your life and you messed it up again.

Patrick Murray

20:78 I talk to myself a lot, but it bothers some people because I use a megaphone.

Steven Wright

20:79 The private papers that Herbert Morrison left behind were so dull and banal that they would provide illumination only if they were burned.

Greg Knight

20:80 Nero renamed the month of April after himself, calling it Neroneus, but the idea never caught on because April is not Neroneus and there is no use pretending that it is.

Will Cuppy

20:81 One day I sat thinking, almost in despair; a hand fell on my shoulder and a voice said reassuringly, 'Cheer up, things could be worse'. So I cheered up, and sure enough, things got worse.

James Hagerty

20:82 I believe in opening my mail once a month – whether it needs it or not.

Bob Considine

20:83 If it weren't for bad luck I wouldn't have any luck at all.
Dick Gregory

20:84 My car had only one previous owner – Coco the clown.
Lenny Windsor

20:85 If I had known I was going to live so long I would have taken better care of myself.
Leon Eldred

20:86 I can only hope that when the enemy reads the list of my officers' names he trembles as I do.
Duke of Wellington

20:87 Some people are always late, like the late King George V.
Spike Milligan

20:88 The object of war is not to die for your country but to make the other bastard die for his.
George Patton

20:89 I'd like to be a procrastinator, but I never seem to get around to it.
Chris Dundee

20:90 Never mistake motion for action.
Ernest Hemingway

20:91 Hard work never killed anybody, but why take a chance on being the first?
Edgar Bergen

20:92 Take the diplomacy out of war and the thing would fall flat in a week.
Will Rogers

20:93 QANTAS is a condom on the penis of progress.
Ian Tuxworth

20:94 I'm about as useful as a one-legged man at an arse-kicking contest.
Dave Dutton

20:95 Neil Armstrong was the first man to walk on the moon. I'm the first man to piss his pants on the moon.
Buzz Aldrin

20:96 They are not really fixing the streets. They are just moving the holes around so the motorists cannot memorise them.

Herb Shriner

20:97 According to my contract, I get fifty dollars from the management every time someone calls me 'nigger'. Please do it again. Let's have the whole audience stand up and do it in unison! I'll retire tomorrow.

Dick Gregory

20:98 I'm gonna be so tough as mayor I'm gonna make Attila the Hun look like a faggot.

Frank Rizzo

20:99 Every place I look at I work out the cubic feet and I say it will make a good warehouse or it won't. Can't help myself. One of the best warehouses I ever did see was the Vatican in Rome.

Arnold Wesker

20:100 Mother Hubbard was old, alone, and a widow – a friendless, old, solitary widow. Yet, did she despair? Did she sit down and weep or read a novel, or wring her hands? No! She went to the cupboard.

Lord Desart

20:101 I have a lot of fun in the summer time. People come up, slap me on the back and I say 'Watch it! My sunburn'. You'd be surprised how many apologies I get.

Dick Gregory

20:102 They couldn't hit an elephant at this dist ...

General Sedgwick

20:103 Drawing on my fine command of language, I said nothing.

Robert Benchley

20:104 It always looks darkest just before it gets totally black.

Charlie Brown

20:105 If you're there before it's over, you're on time.

James J. Walker

20:106 Mick Jagger has big lips. I once saw him suck an egg out of a chicken.

Joan Rivers

20:107 The Royal Navy – rum, sodomy, and the lash.

Winston Churchill

20:108 Would you like to find out what it's like to be a member of a minority group? Try putting in an honest day's work occasionally.

Kelly Fordyce

20:109 Epitaph for a dead waiter – God finally caught his eye.

George S. Kaufman

20:110 A lot of people have been asking why there are no Negro astronauts. Well, I've got a surprise for you. One of those seven boys is. He's just looked white since they told him what he volunteered for.

Dick Gregory

20:111 Never play leapfrog with a unicorn.

Michael Shea

20:112 William F. Buckley looks and sounds not unlike Hitler – but without the charm.

Gore Vidal

20:113 It's great to be with Bill Buckley, because you don't have to think. He takes a position and you automatically take the opposite one and you know you're right.

J.K. Galbraith

20:114 You had to stand in line to hate Harry Cohn.

Hedda Hopper

20:115 I have my standards. They may be low, but I have them.

Bette Midler

20:116 The trouble with doing nothing is that you can never take any time off.

Hoagy Carmichael

20:117 There is no limit to how complicated things can get, on account of one thing always leading to another.

E.B. White

20:118 If it's not one thing, it's two.

James Ledford

20:119 I have never killed a man, but I have read many obituaries with a lot of pleasure.

Clarence Darrow

20:120 No issue is so small that it can't be blown out of proportion.
Stuart Hughes

20:121 More than any time in history mankind faces a crossroads. One path leads to despair and utter hopelessness, the other to total destruction. Let us pray that we have the wisdom to choose correctly.

Woody Allen

20:122 I have a memory like an elephant. In fact elephants often consult me.

Noel Coward

20:123 I was going to buy a copy of *The Power of Positive Thinking* and then I thought 'What the hell good would that do?'
Ronald Shakes

20:124 Too bad that all the people who know how to run the country are busy driving taxicabs or cutting hair.
George Burns

20:125 He must have had a magnificent build before his stomach went in for a career of its own.

Margaret Halsley

20:126 I had to give up masochism – I was enjoying it too much.
Mel Calman

20:127 The pen is mightier than the sword – and considerably easier to write with.

Marty Feldman

20:128 E.W.B. Nicholson, Bodley's Librarian, spent three days at the London Docks, watching outgoing ships, after losing a book at the Bodley, which was afterwards discovered slightly out of place on the shelf.

Falconer Madan

20:129 A diplomat is a person who can tell you to go to hell in such a way that you actually look forward to the trip.
Caskie Stinnet

20:130 What was the war like? My dear fellow it was awful – the noise, and the people!

W.H. Auden

20:131 The first think I do in the morning is to read the obituaries in *The Times* and if I am not in them I get up.

Noel Coward

20:132 In the battle of wits, Frank Fay entered the skirmish almost totally unarmed.

Milton Berle

20:133 I hate the poor and look forward eagerly to their extermination.

George Bernard Shaw

20:134 Anything that man says you've got to take with a dose of salts.

Samuel Goldwyn

20:135 Have you ever noticed that wrong numbers are never engaged?

Steven Wright

20:136 Whenever I feel like exercise, I lie down until the feeling passes.

R.M. Hutchins

20:137 When I was young, I was told: 'You'll see, when you're fifty.' I am fifty and I haven't seen a thing.

Eric Satie

20:138 I once had a rose named after me and I was very flattered. But I was not pleased to read the description in the catalogue: no good in a bed, but fine up against a wall.

Eleanor Roosevelt

20:139 Auntie did you feel no pain
Falling from that apple tree?
Would you do it, please again,
'Cos my friend here didn't see?

Harry Graham

20:140 Watch out when you're getting all you want: only hogs being fattened for the slaughter get all they want.

Joel Chandler Harris

20:141 There is no more agreeable spectacle than to observe an old friend fall from a roof-top.

Confucius

20:142 Saturday morning, although recurring at regular and well foreseen intervals, always seems to take Baker Street Station by surprise.

W.S. Gilbert

20:143 Never make excuses, never let them see you bleed, and never get separated from your baggage.

Wesley Price

20:144 They made me a present of Mornington Crescent – they threw it a brick at a time.

Albert Chevalier

20:145 I don't know what my dog's real name is but I call him 'Rover'.

Stafford Beer

20:146 A Jewish nymphomaniac is a woman who will make love with a man the same day she has her hair done.

Maureen Lipman

20:147 Middle age is when you are sitting at home on a Saturday night and the telephone rings and you hope it isn't for you.

Ogden Nash

20:148 The method preferred by most balding men for making themselves look silly is called the 'comb-over' which is when the man grows the hair on one side of his head very long and combs it across the bald area, creating an effect that looks from the top like an egg in the grasp of a large tropical spider.

Dave Barry

20:149 I got some new underwear the other day. Well, new to me.

Emo Philips

20:150 Who invented the brush they put next to the toilet? That thing hurts.

Andy Andrews

20:151 It's a small world, but I wouldn't like to have to paint it.

Steven Wright

20:152 If you've got them by the balls, their hearts and minds will follow.

John Wayne

20:153 The answer is in the plural and they bounce.

Edwin Lutyens

20:154 My neighbour asked if he could use my lawnmower and I told him of course he could so long as he didn't take it out of my garden.

Eric Morecambe

20:155 A collision is what happens when two motorists go after the same pedestrian.

Bob Newhart

20:156 I have so much to do that I am going to bed.

Robert Benchley

20:157 'Victorian Apartment' means that the bedrooms have only enough space for one tightly bound woman.

Wes Smith

INDEX

209

Critchley, Julian, 7:44
Cronenberg, David, 9:115
Crosbie, Paddy,12:44
Crosland, T.W., 13:43
Crow, Frank, 11:29
Crowley, Alastair, 1:22
Cummings, e.e., 2:52, 7:28
Cuomo, Mario, 2:89
Cuppy, Will, 9:6, 9:20, 20:80
Curran, John Philpot, 11:102
Curtis, Tony, 9:142
Cvikota, Raymond J., 2:54

Dali, Slavador, 1:8, 1:19, 9:279
Dane, Frank, 14:99
Dangerfield, Rodney, 5:15, 8:29, 8:106, 8:165, 9:12, 9:238, 18:35, 20:17
Darlington, W.A., 19:52
Darrow, Clarence, 14:163, 20:119
D'Aumale, Henri Duc, 9:233
Dawson, Les' (Mother), 19:2
Dawson, Les, 8:94, 8:146, 9:72, 9:96, 20:19
Da Vinci, Leonardo, 9:45
Davies, Jack, 9:261
Davies, Robertson, 4:54, 5:37
Davis, Michael, 2:95
Davis, Bette, 9:22, 9:141, 10:8
Davis, Michael, 2:95
Davis, Steve, 18:85
Day, Clarence S., 17:61
Day, Lilian, 9:13
De Cervantes, Miguel, 9:256
Deford, Frank, 10:73
De Generis, Ellen, 8:85
De Goncourt, Edmond, 5:9
De La Bruyere, Jean, 11:101
De Manio, Jack, 10:34
De Meur, Tony, 9:33
Dent, Alan, 12:19
De Quincey, Thomas, 6:20
Desart, Lord, 20:100
De Vega-Carpio, L.F., 7:87
De Vere White, Terence,14:97
De Vries, Peter, 8:14, 9:123
De Witt, George, 7:34
Diabolus, Dick, 9:108, 12:2

Dickens, Charles, 2:36
Dietz, Howard, 12:50
Diller, Phyllis, 2:80, 3:59, 4:29, 5:35, 8:2, 8:15, 8:79, 8:82, 8:124, 8:141, 9:86, 9:131, 9:164, 9:245, 9:248, 11:83
Dillon, James, 14:19
Dirksen, Everett, 2:70
Disraeli, Benjamin, 7:27, 7:38, 11:100, 14:28, 15:85
Dix, Dorothy, 9:43
Dobie, J.F., 4:13
Dodd, Ken, 4:8, 11:60, 11:70
Donleavy, J.P., 13:77
Donovan, James, 15:52
Doonican, Val, 18:105
Drake, Francis, 18:42
Driver, Christopher, 5:5
Duchamp, Marcel, 1:25
Duffecy, James, 15:94
Duke, Winifred, 6:32
Dumas, Alexandre, 9:92
Dundee, Chris, 20:89
Dunne, Finley Peter, 2:33, 18:21, 20:75
Duppa, Richard, 11:86
Durante, Jimmy, 8:53
Durrell, Lawrence, 4:32, 17:47
Durst, Will, 9:57, 14:113
Dutton, Dave, 3:37, 9:184, 20:94

Eastwood, Clint, 20:65
Eaton, Hal, 10:71
Eckland, Britt, 9:192
Edwards, Bob, 14:20
Edwards, Oliver, 15:24
Ehrlich, Paul, 16:37
Eisenhower, Dwight D., 15:21
Eldin, Peter, 9:260
Eldred, Leon, 20:85
Eliot, Charles W., 4:26
Eliot, T.S., 7:12, 7:95
Elliot, John, 13:87
Ellis, H.F., 16:3, 16:7
Elson, Frank, 9:272
Elton, Lord, 5:34
Emerson, R.W., 17:36
Ephron, Nora, 7:55

211

Hudson, Christopher, 11:93
Hughes, Edward, 13:56
Hughes, Rupert,9:54
Hughes, Stuart, 20:120
Hume, John14:133
Humphreys, Emyr, 10:95
Humphries, Barry, 13:94, 13:97
Hunt, Lamar, 6:38
Hunt, Leigh, 5:33
Hunter, Keith Allan, 17:91
Hurst, Geoff, 18:126
Hurst, Gerald, 2:86
Huston, David, 14:126
Hutchins, R.M., 4:47, 20:136
Huxley, Aldous, 9:109, 11:30, 15:64
Hynes, Michael, 10:44

Imhoff, John, 2:37
Imlach, Punch, 18:68
Ince, W.R., 7:23
Inge, Dean, 14:138, 15:67, 15:71
Ingersoll, Robert G., 8:33
Ingram, Kay, 2:78
Ingrams, Richard, 10:86, 17:16
Irving, Henry, 7:79

Jackson, Andrew, 14:127
James, Clive, 10:30, 14:34, 14:101, 14:149
James I, King, 7:21
Jeffery, Francis, 16:35
Jeffries, Lambert, 17:37
Jellinek, Roger, 14:35
Jenkins, Clive, 2:53
Jerome, Jerome K., 19:21, 20:8
Jerome, Saint, 2:84
Jerrold, Douglas, 9:145
Jit, Inder, 14:102
John, Elton,9:35
Johnson, Lyndon B., 2:71, 14:3, 14:4, 14:41, 14:85
Johnson, P.G., 15:72
Johnson, Samuel, 5:2, 7:2, 7:11, 7:39, 8:20, 11:110, 13:5, 13:23, 13:33, 13:38, 15:20, 17:63, 18:30, 20:1, 20:35
Jones, Bill, 20:58

Jones, Bryn, 8:120
Jones, C.T., 2:7
Jones, Franklin Pierce, 9:171, 11:40
Jong, Erica, 9:50
Jordan, Steve, 18:99
Joyce, James, 7:9, 15:28
Joyce, Nora, 7:62
Jung, Carl, 11:64
Juvenal, 8:148

Kahn, Sammy, 12:51
Kalin, Mike, 5:47
Kapp, Karl, 16:27
Kapusta, Richard, 16:32
Kasspe, Arthur, 20:62
Katz, Jonathan, 9:291
Kavanagh, Patrick, 9:40, 13:34
Kavanagh, Ted, 9:182
Kaufman, George S., 2:22, 20:109
Kaufmann, Max, 7:103, 9:282
Kauffmann, Stanley, 19:28
Keane, J.B., 4:40, 15:38
Keegan, William, 14:73
Keillor, Garrison, 8:83, 8:115, 13:89
Kelly, Jack, 18:31
Kempton, Murray, 14:115
Kendal, Margaret, 19:41
Kennedy, C., 9:198
Kerr, Alphonse, 7:83
Kerr, Jean, 8:75, 11:15, 17:57
Kerry, John, 14:132
Kersh, Gerald, 9:191
Keynes, J.M., 2:90
Kierkegaard, Soren, 9:262
Kingsley, Ben, 10:43
Kingston, Miles, 2:10
Kinnock, Neil, 14:98
Kinsey, Mrs Alfred, 9:104
Kipling, Rudyard, 9:124
Kirkland, Lane, 3:43
Kissinger, Henry, 13:69, 14:95, 14:111, 14:147
Klein, Gene, 6:37
Knebel, Fletcher, 16:19
Knight, Greg, 14:79, 20:79
Knoll, Erwin, 10:9
Knott, Blanche, 5:12, 6:18

217

220

The Bumper Book of Kerryman Jokes

Des MacHale

How do you recognise a Kerryman with a double-barrelled name?
He signs himself X-X.

Why did most Kerrymen paint their doors in 1979?
They heard the Pope was coming to Knock.

What did the Kerryman say when he slipped on a bar of soap?
That's life boy.

How do you sink a Kerry submarine?
Knock on the door.

How do you recognise a Kerry bank?
The key is under the mat.

What did the Kerry postman get on his first day working?
The sack.

Have you heard about the Kerryman who had a heart transplant?
He sent a get-well card to the donor.

What notice would you see outside a Kerry church?
Closed on Sundays.

How do you recognise a Kerry real estate salesman?
He carries his samples in his fingernails.

Letters of a Matchmaker

John B. Keane

These are the letters of a country matchmaker faithfully recorded by John B. Keane, whose knowledge of match-making is second to none.

In these letters is revealed the unquenchable, insatiable longing that smoulders unseen under the mute, impassive faces of our bachelor brethren.

Comparisons may be odious but readers will find it fascinating to contrast the Irish matchmaking system with that of the 'Cumangettum Love Parlour' in Philadelphia. They will meet many unique characters from the Judas Jennies of New York to Fionnuala Crust of Coomasahara who buried two giant-sized, sexless husbands but eventually found happiness with a pint-sized jockey from North Cork.

Letters of a Country Postman

John B. Keane

'Steam is a powerful weapon ... if you have a sufficiency of curiosity and cunning. You can read the minds of your neighbours with steam. You can discover their innermost thoughts and secret yearnings and the progress of their off-spring and kinsfolk in distant places ...'

Katie the Steamer and her niece Sister Gabrielle 'sit in the kitchen and Katie reveals all that there is to be known about the fortunes of the people of the postal district of Ballyfee. To the casual listener it sounds as if a litany is being recited with the nun offering short responses every so often. What she really is doing is egging Katie on when she hesitates before the juicier parts of her revelations ...'

Dictionary of Irish Quotations

Sean Sheehan

Dictionary of Irish Quotations contains a highly enjoyable and varied selection of interesting, informative, intriguing, infuriating – and sometimes just witty – remarks made by Irish people on a number of topical subjects. The quotations included range from the fifth century to today and from the classical to the colloquial. There are over 150 authors – from St Brigid to Sinéad O'Connor. Yeats and Swift are quoted here and Wilde and Joyce. So too are Maria Edgeworth and Mary Lavin; Robert Emmet and Roger Casement; Douglas Hyde and Mary Robinson; Sean Hughes and Neil Jordan ...

Entries are grouped under subject headings, with both an author index and a first line index, making this *Dictionary of Irish Quotations* readily accessible to all readers.

'... Before the Devil Knows You're Dead'
Irish Blessings, Toasts and Curses

Padraic o'Farrell

Hearing news of a death or marriage, consoling neighbours in sorrow or sharing their joy, looking for a husband or wife, saving turf or going fishing – Irish people had blessings and curses for every occasion. Luckily many of the old sayings have survived. A few startling new ones have been added too!